GOOD
MORNING,
OLIVE

GOOD MORNING, OLIVE

Haunted Theatres
of Broadway and Beyond

Robert Viagas

APPLAUSE
THEATRE & CINEMA BOOKS

ESSEX, CONNECTICUT

APPLAUSE
THEATRE & CINEMA BOOKS

An imprint of Globe Pequot, the trade division of
The Rowman & Littlefield Publishing Group, Inc.
4501 Forbes Blvd., Ste. 200
Lanham, MD 20706
www.rowman.com

Distributed by NATIONAL BOOK NETWORK

Library of Congress Cataloging-in-Publication Data Available

ISBN: 978-1-4930-6453-3 (cloth : alk. paper)
ISBN: 978-1-4930-6454-0 (electronic)

♾️™ The paper used in this publication meets the minimum requirements of American
National Standard for Information Sciences—Permanence of Paper for Printed Library
Materials, ANSI/NISO Z39.48-1992.

For my beloved Donna Martin Viagas, who patiently read through every word and was scarily full of great suggestions.

Special Thanks:

Dana Amendola, The Shubert Archive, Annemarie van Roessel at the New York Public Library/Billy Rose Collection, Mark Lamos, Howard Sherman, Thomas Stein, John Darby, Disney Theatricals, Dennis Crowley, the Shubert Organization, John Cerullo, Ray Venezia, Elissa Blake, Mark Shenton, Tripp Phillips, Joan Marcus, my agent Susan H. Schulman, and the Applause Books team, editor Chris Chappell, Laurel Myers, and Barbara Claire.

But most of all, the many actors, stagehands, janitors, audience members and other theatre folk who shared their stories with me.

Sections of this book were published previously in Encore Monthly *magazine and* Playbill.

Time is empty air.

To be or nobody.

All theatres are haunted . . .

—David Van Tiegham via Mac Wellman, *Crowbar*

Contents

Preface

Hamlet calls death "the undiscovered country from whose bourn no traveler returns."

But he's wrong. Some do return.

Each night after the applause dies, the curtain falls, the audience vanishes, the cleaners dust and the lights are killed, great theatres become dark and silent places.

But not always quite empty.

That's when the theatre ghosts make their entrance and strut and fret their hour upon the shadowed stage. Many of Broadway's busiest theatres continue to be just as busily haunted by spirits, some with well-known names and histories.

Good Morning, Olive is about the ghosts who haunt theatres on Broadway and around the world.

Broadway is the playground of stars, so it's probably not surprising to learn that even its ghosts are stars. Let's meet some of Broadway's best known—and most active—celebrity ghosts. Don't worry: like Casper, they tend to be friendly . . . for the most part.

There's something special about theatres, something especially conducive and welcoming to ghosts. Charles J. Adams III wrote, "By its very nature, a theatre is a vault within which every human emotion is at once imprisoned, impersonated, imitated, and elicited. Tangles of cords and ropes . . . tall curtains and backdrops which fade into high darkness . . . cubicles and trap doors and passageways."

With that in mind, on the first day of rehearsal for each of his shows, Tony Award–winning star Brian Stokes Mitchell calls his fellow actors to the stage. He asks them to remember all the performers who have walked the same boards down through the decades, and who have left a little of their energy soaked into the very beams and boards of each theatre.

Sometimes they leave more than that.

After cemeteries, theatres are some of the most extensively haunted places on earth—at least according to the volumes of stories and anecdotes, some known to the public, others passed from person to person among the brotherhood of backstage workers. Theatre people take these stories seriously. There's even a tradition of never leaving a theatre completely dark. Every night, before a theatre is locked, a stagehand places on stage a piece of equipment known as the Ghost Light—usually just a bare bulb on an upright stand. In his autobiography, titled *Ghost Light*, former *New York Times* critic Frank Rich said there is a superstition that if an emptied theatre is ever left completely dark, a ghost will take up residence. To prevent this, the ghost light is left burning at center stage after the audience and all of the actors and musicians have gone home. For theatres already haunted, it's there to keep the resident poltergeists from doing too much mischief.

Good Morning, Olive shines its light on some of the best-known of these ghosts, and shares backstage stories of hauntings from the past and a surprisingly large number still carrying on today. This book takes its title from the words that actors working at Broadway's New Amsterdam Theatre say— today still—when they enter the theatre's stage door on West 41st Street. They are greeting the ghost of Olive Thomas, Ziegfeld showgirl and, briefly, a silent movie star, who committed suicide (or was she murdered?) at the dawn of the Roaring Twenties. A century later, she is still such a presence at the theatre—appearing almost exclusively to men—that her photo is posted at every entrance to the "New Am," as the people who work there call it. And they can tell Olive is listening. Those who fail to greet her sometimes find personal articles thrown across their dressing rooms, makeup lights blinking on and off, or important items missing altogether. Her life (and death) story, as told in this book in its complete form for the first time, may be a real-life murder mystery waiting to be solved.

A lot of the stories in this book are murder mysteries. Most hauntings begin with intense passion of one kind or another. In some cases, they're just the result of a person being bitten by the "theatre bug" so hard that the obsession continues beyond the grave.

Not all the stories are terrifying. Some theatre folk draw great comfort from their ghosts. Far from being frightened of them, many feel they are benevolent beings, intermediaries to the Great Beyond, offering solace or keeping silent company to the living.

By the way, you may notice that I will rarely cite ghost-hunting TV shows. For the most part they make a great fuss over very little. Toting all kinds of useless technology, the hosts react melodramatically to every creak, and often to nothing at all. Not one show I've ever seen has presented an unmistakably clear photo or video of a ghost.

Like Olive, a number of the ghosts in this book are mischievous, especially if not placated in one way or another, and a few are indeed malicious if not outright evil. These "ghoulies and ghosties and long-leggedy beasties" produce grim and frightening visages. These are the revenants of people who met a bad end, or who left behind some unfinished business and have an axe to grind. One is a harbinger of death, another offers a foreshadowing of failure, yet another group of ghosts died together in a horrible disaster.

All are, by definition, dramatic, and their stories haunt these pages.

WHAT EXACTLY ARE GHOSTS?

Most mainstream religions make no allowance for ghosts. Where they acknowledge them at all, they are regarded as phantasms or hallucinations woven by the devil. This gives rise to the common belief that they don't exist at all. But so many people have seen or experienced *something*—often the same *something* that others have seen, too. So, what could they be?

There are a lot of theories. Most, but not all, see them as manifestations of the human spirit, a residue of life that is eternal—or at least more durable than the body. It is believed to have ended its time on earth and, en route to another plane of existence, for some reason, became stuck on this one.

There's the trauma theory: A sudden accident or crime sends the soul smash-cutting into death before its appointed time. It exists in a twilight zone between the living world and the next one. No wonder these ghosts are often frightening. They've gone mad in an existential limbo, and they hate the world to which they no longer have full access. But sometimes they find they can grasp just a tiny, frustrating, malicious bit of that world. These are known—to the living—as hauntings. Less frequently, these ghosts aren't insane or evil at all. They still love the world, or at least take pity on it, and intervene (when they can) in benevolent ways.

Then there's the photographic theory: a ghost is not a soul at all. It is an image of a person or incident that was so powerfully vivid that it leaves its recurring image stamped on the fabric of space-time itself. This theory of ghosts interprets them as a frightening image, but one that has no real power to harm or help us.

Some people believe that a ghost is a soul who doesn't realize it is dead and behaves as if it is still alive—though sometimes expressing confusion that things don't work normally anymore. They can scare the pants off you, but they themselves don't understand why.

Or if the ghost does realize it is dead, it hangs around because it has some unfinished business—a curse to deliver or remove, someone to punish, some wrong to be righted.

Or perhaps a ghost is a soul that has no unfinished business but, for one reason or another, is unable or *not yet ready* to move on to the afterlife. The period is described by Thornton Wilder in *Our Town*, as "waitin' for the eternal part in them to come out clear."

Science fiction offers yet another fanciful theory: ghosts have crossed over from another dimension. The moment of death opens a portal like an aneurysm between worlds, allowing us to glimpse what's happening there—or even do more. The stage opens less supernatural portals every time they whisk us to another time and place. Perhaps some of these portals linger and enable us to glimpse shadows of other worlds.

It makes as much sense as any of the other theories.

But there is one more answer, and I suspect it pertains to many theatre ghosts in particular. These ghosts fall into none of the above categories; rather, they simply have become so profoundly and extraordinarily attached to a place—the theatre—which they labored all their lives to get into, that they never wish to leave.

Ever.

As Stephen Sondheim put it in *West Side Story*, "Even death won't part us now."

And why shouldn't this syndrome affect theatre ghosts especially? Ghosts are very theatrical. They have a great deal in common with old-time vaudeville performers. In the era before radio and TV, and long before YouTube and TikTok, vaudeville performers would put together an "act"—a skit, a song, a display of some special talent—and perform it over and over, in performance after performance (sometimes several shows a day) in city after city, sometimes for years. The same with most ghosts. Like most vaudevillians, ghosts always wear the same "costumes." They look the same (e.g., vaudeville alum Groucho Marx's mustache) and perform the same actions in the same places, apparently for eternity.

TYPES OF GHOSTS

While they are all classified as ghosts, these spirits come in several different forms. All flavors make appearances in this book, in one theatre or another.

The lowest-level haunt is manifested by an eerie feeling. The hair may stand up on the back of your head for no apparent reason. You experience an undeniable sensation of dread, or, less commonly, of heavenly well-being and safety.

Still low on the totem pole is the common house poltergeist. The word is German for "knocking spirit," and it's an apt name. They are the "things that go bump in the night"—ghosts that make noises and sometimes even move or change things, but never materialize. They are the ghosts that sound like someone squeaking up the stairs to your room, but when you go to check, no one is there. They are the ghosts who leave open cabinets you know you closed. They shove things off tables. They shift furniture. They may pull your hair, or make it feel like someone has gotten into bed with you, when you know you are alone.

But most of all, they knock on things, which is where they get their name.

The next-strongest manifestation is the ice-cold cloud that seems to materialize out of nowhere. Sometimes the cloud has a color, but the cold inside these clouds imparts more than just a physical sensation. It makes your soul cold.

Moving further into the visual is the disembodied shadow, also called a shade. Shadows are creepy enough, but when they detach from their owner, as in the first scene of *Peter Pan*, they can be very disturbing, especially when they start following you.

Moving up again, we come to perhaps the most familiar: the Casper-the-Friendly-Ghost-type wispy white ghost, the kind you can make as a Halloween costume by poking eye holes in an old sheet.

But not all of these "white sheet" ghosts appear as mere smoke or otherworldly vapor. They can also appear as a full-color body or body part: a face, hand, torso, or pair of eyes. In one case I found a ghost who manifested as nothing but a pair of feet. Feet are very rare, even among full-color ghosts. People who have seen these real-seeming revenants say they tend to fade out below the waist.

But some don't, which brings us to the Business Class level of ghost-dom: ghosts who look like fully articulated, live, human beings. Living people who see them often believe at first that they are in the presence of another living person, like themselves. But silent.

Finally we arrive at the top level of theatre ghosts, and ghosts in general: those who speak and even touch. Sometimes they say the same thing over and over. Or shriek. Rarer still are the ones that have a conversation with the living person.

All these are found lurking in the dark backstage hallways of the world's theatres.

Let's meet them.

THE NEW AMSTERDAM THEATRE

OLIVE THOMAS'S DEATH

"I've taken poison!"

Olive Thomas stumbled back to her bathroom in the Hôtel Ritz in Paris, where the pretty, young actress was on a second honeymoon with her husband, Jack Pickford, brother of silent-movie sweetheart Mary Pickford. It was 1920, and these were among her last words, because, after a night of partying, she had just downed an overdose of her husband's toxic medicine instead of aspirin. The official cause of death would later be listed as "acute nephritis caused by accidental poisoning," but it's hard to accidentally swallow the better part of bottle of pills, which just happened to be shaped like little coffins.

Olive died five days later, and her body was brought back across the Atlantic to Woodlawn Cemetery in the Bronx for burial.

"Good morning, Olive." That's what actors working at Broadway's New Amsterdam Theatre say—today still in 2022—when they enter the theatre's stage door on West 41st Street. They are greeting the ghost

The marquee of Broadway's New Amsterdam Theatre. Photo by Robert Viagas

of Olive, a featured *Ziegfeld Follies* showgirl and, briefly, a silent movie star, who lost her life at the dawn of the Roaring Twenties. A century later she is still such a presence at the theatre that her photo is posted at every entrance to the "New Am," as the people who work there call it.

And they can tell Olive is listening.

Olive has a complex personality for a ghost. Like the star she was, she demands respect. She can be flirtatious with men and supportive of women. But if she feels she's been slighted, well, look out. Those who fail to greet her sometimes find personal articles thrown across their dressing room, makeup lights blinking on an off, or important items missing altogether. She has also shown the ability to move heavy equipment.

Olive had something of an *Unsinkable Molly Brown* upbringing, rising from the bottom of the social ladder to the top. She was born Oliveretta Elain Duffy on October 20, 1894, in Charleroi, Pennsylvania, an industrial suburb of what was then the nation's steelmaking center, Pittsburgh.

After an unpleasant childhood, she married very young to Bernard Krug Thomas, an older man who worked as a clerk at the Pressed Steel Car Company. He still lived with his parents and, after they married on April 1, 1911, so did she. It was not a happy marriage. Oliveretta quickly realized that the blue-collar life in western Pennsylvania was not for her. She was struck with that familiar yearning to be "up where the people are, up where the talkin' is, up where the jokes goin' on." Everyone she met told her she was the prettiest girl in Charleroi, and that doubtless made her wonder if she could make a splash just as big in a bigger place—maybe even the biggest place of all back then—New York!

At the age of sixteen, she packed her suitcase, left her husband, and headed to the Big Apple to seek her fortune, with dreams of becoming a fashion model like the ones she saw in magazines. It's an old story, but this one would take more twists than most. Years later, after Olive's brilliant success, her ex-husband gave a mournful interview to the Pittsburg Press, saying his wife left him because of her desire to obtain a life of "luxury," and to "improve her station."

She lived for a time at her cousin's apartment in Harlem, working in retail. People kept telling her how beautiful she was, so she entered "The Most Beautiful Girl in New York City" contest run by the celebrated commercial artist Howard Chandler Christy—and won! She shortened her name to Olive Thomas and modeled for another famous artist, Harrison Fisher, and wound up on the cover of the *Saturday Evening Post*. Fisher, who had spent a lot of time looking at her, declared publicly that Olive was simply "the most beautiful girl in the world."

This came in an era when a woman's worth was closely tied to her attractiveness to men. Many women (and some men) were fighting against that notion. In 1920, the year Olive died, the Nineteenth Amendment was added to the Constitution, giving women the right to vote. But little in women's day-to-day treatment changed. Whatever else they may have accomplished in life, their looks were still their main currency in the world at large. But in that world—the living world that she would never want to leave—Olive was considered by many to be the pinnacle of womanhood.

Through Fisher, Olive came to the attention of that era's Jeff Bezos, Florenz Ziegfeld, master of the spectacular *Ziegfeld Follies* stage revues, which came out with a new edition each year.

"Flo" Ziegfeld (that's "feld" not "field") was always on the lookout for the best singers, the funniest comedians, the hottest songwriters, and the most fashionable designers. He offered them the industry's top dollar for their services. He was also perpetually on the prowl for pretty girls (only) to line up behind those stars and tap to those pop hits, while displaying those costumes. "Ziegfeld Girls" weren't treated like other chorus girls. They were treated as artists and models. They were sought after by wealthy men who showered them with expensive gifts in return for their company. They wore the title "Ziegfeld Girl" with pride, and continued to do so into the twenty-first century by helping launch the Ziegfeld Club, now an organization to support young professional women who are making careers in theatre.

Flo Ziegfeld saw Olive Thomas, and there was fire.

The *Midnight Frolic*

Ziegfeld didn't put her in the *Follies* proper right away. He had another plan. The *Follies* were playing at the main stage on the main floor of the New Amsterdam. But that wasn't the only theatre in the building. Remember that this was 1915. In the years before air-conditioning, many theatres opened what were known as "roof gardens" where shows could be performed on an outdoor stage for an open-air audience hoping for a breeze. The space known as the New Amsterdam Roof was a purpose-built "roof" theatre, within the walls of the building, but with a retractable roof that could be opened or closed, solving the inevitable weather problem.

The New Amsterdam Roof was the venue chosen by Ziegfeld for his special *secondary* show, the musical revue the *Ziegfeld Midnight Frolic*, which offered willing adults a slightly more R-rated experience than they could get downstairs. As the title indicates, performances had the glittery Ziegfeld touch, but began at the racy hour of midnight, after the regular *Follies* folk had packed up for the evening.

Olive became one of the most buzzed-about starlets of the 1915 edition of the *Midnight Frolic*. In one scene she wore a filmy peplos drape like that of a Greek goddess. Another was an outfit made of nothing but balloons. She would dance among the male patrons who were permitted to pop the balloons with their lit cigars. Suitors lined up, showering her with gems and furs. When her belongings were auctioned after her death, the list of jewelry was jaw-dropping: sapphires, pearls, jade, gold, platinum, and a blizzard of diamonds of every configuration and description.

Master pinup artist Alberto Vargas asked to use her as a model in one of his erotic paintings, *Memories of Olive*. It depicted her nude from the waist up, her head thrown back, sniffing a rose and clutching one breast. Ziegfeld bought the painting and hung it in his office at the New Amsterdam, much to the displeasure of his wife, Billie Burke. It's believed that Olive and Flo were sometimes intimate during her *Follies* period, which also didn't endear Olive to Burke.

The space once known as the New Amsterdam Roof Theatre is still there, now remodeled as the offices of Disney Theatricals. Executive Director Tom Schumacher's desk now sits somewhere close to where Olive once danced. And perhaps sometimes still does.

It didn't take long before this dazzling nymph came to the attention of Hollywood. Much to Ziegfeld's distress, Myron Selznick signed her to an exclusive contract for his budding studio, Selznick Pictures, and Olive packed again, this time for the West Coast.

The Selznicks kept her busy. Olive made twenty-four movies—all silents, of course—from 1916 to 1920. These included *The Follies Girl* and *Prudence on Broadway* to capitalize on her stage fame, *The Spite Bride*, and to reflect her new "station" in the world, *Limousine Life*, *Youthful Folly*, and *The Flapper*. Her last film was poignantly titled *Everybody's Sweetheart*. Interestingly, she is credited with having written the story for *Youthful Folly*.

Having risen so far so fast from misery, she now floated through her glamorous new life like a speared olive in a martini.

As the latest and brightest bauble on the Hollywood Christmas tree, Olive immediately drew the inevitable attention of the male wolves in the movie colony. After some jostling, the prize was claimed in 1916 by Jack Pickford, the ne'er-do-well younger brother of period superstar Mary Pickford. For her many silent film appearances, Mary had previously earned the sobriquet "America's Sweetheart," so she understood the kind of adulation Olive inspired. But, though they had jobs in the same industry and became sisters-in-law, they never became close. Was Olive's *Everybody's Sweetheart* a jab at Mary's "America's Sweetheart"? There was some rivalry there, especially over Jack.

In addition to her acting career, Mary Pickford became a powerful producer, one of the cofounders of Pickford–Fairbanks Studios and United Artists (with Charlie Chaplin). She was also one of the founders of the Academy of Motion Picture Arts and Sciences, which administers the Oscars. Mary's brother Jack had a modest career as an actor, but he flung himself at life as a handsome playboy and lived in his sister's shadow. Still, to marry into the Pickford family, as Olive did, was to marry into the royal family of Hollywood. In this case, "Queen" Mary didn't really approve. In her 1955 autobiography, *Sunshine and Shadow*,

Mary Pickford remembered her late sister-in-law, whom she nicknamed "Ollie," writing,

> I regret to say that none of us [Pickfords] approved of the marriage at that time. Mother thought Jack was too young, and Lottie and I felt that Olive, being in musical comedy, belonged to an alien world. Ollie had all the rich, eligible men of the social world at her feet. She had been deluged with proposals from her own world of the theatre as well. Which was not at all surprising. The beauty of Olive Thomas is legendary. The girl had the loveliest violet-blue eyes I have ever seen. They were fringed with long dark lashes that seemed darker because of the delicate translucent pallor of her skin. I could understand why Florenz Ziegfeld never forgave Jack for taking her away from the Follies. She and Jack were madly in love with one another, but I always thought of them as a couple of children playing together.

Jack and Olive's life together was indeed like something out of an F. Scott Fitzgerald novel. In addition to the drinking and fast living, there were the inevitable furious spats, breakups, and ardent reconciliations. In 1920, they decided to rededicate themselves to their marriage by taking a second honeymoon to Paris. It was there, in a moment that was supposed to be so happy and affirming, that Olive discovered Jack had contracted syphilis from someone outside their marriage. Worse, he had passed it on to her.

Penicillin, the first of the family of powerful antibiotics still used today, wouldn't be invented until 1928, and wouldn't be widely administered as a treatment for infection until World War II. In 1920, the best treatment available was mercury bichloride, a highly corrosive compound used to process chemicals and develop photography film. In controlled doses it was also prescribed as an antibiotic to treat stubborn infections, including syphilis. But the medicine form was so toxic that it was sold in dark blue bottles with the word "poison" in bigger letters than "Mercury Bichloride." If that wasn't enough, the bottle also had a red skull-and-crossbones on it, like a pirate flag. And if that still wasn't enough, the mottled dark blue pills were shaped like little coffins. Each pill had a skull-and-crossbones stamped on one side and, in capital letters, the word "POISON" stamped on the other side.

Pickford brought this medicine along on his trip so he could treat himself between shows and parties.

There are many versions of what happened on September 5, 1920. The closest we have to a first-person account of the night Olive took the pills comes again from Mary Pickford's autobiography.

I cannot blame the majority of people who know the case only from the lurid newspaper accounts of the time for believing that Olive Thomas committed suicide. Yet I am ready to take an oath that Ollie's death was an accident. Jack told me so and Jack would not have lied to me.

Moreover, what he said was fully corroborated by several details of the tragedy itself.

The night of Olive's death in Paris she and Jack had been doing the night spots. At one o'clock Jack insisted on taking Ollie back to their hotel, since they were leaving at seven that morning by plane for London.

They were already undressed when a crowd of friends trooped in, scolding them for breaking up the party and ordering them back into their clothes to continue making the rounds until dawn. Jack said he was too tired. The crowd finally left. Jack went to bed and Ollie started to write a letter to her mother, outlining their future plans. The unfinished letter was still on the desk after she was taken to the hospital.

Jack awakened with the light in his eyes, surprised to see Ollie still up. "Please come to bed darling," he said. "It's so late and I can't sleep with that light on."

Ollie answered petulantly. "You don't care that I can't sleep, do you? I've got an awful headache."

Ollie turned out the lights and went to the window overlooking the street.

"Why don't you take an aspirin?" Jack said, and went back to sleep. Again he was awakened, this time by a crash and a scream. Ollie was standing in the darkened bathroom. Jack rushed to her side.

"Quick, Jack," she said, "turn the light on and see if the bottle with the bichloride of mercury tablets is in the cabinet?"

Jack looked and said, "No, Ollie; only the aspirin bottle is here."

Olive gave another scream. "Then I've taken poison!"

Ollie had put the mercury tablets somewhere else, but the maid had evidently placed the bottles, which were the same size, side by side on the shelf of the medicine cabinet. Jack tried to wash out Ollie's stomach by giving her twelve to fifteen glasses of tepid water. Then he dashed downstairs to secure melted butter and milk. But everything was tightly locked, kitchens and ice boxes, and no one was around but the night watchman. After a frantic search Jack obtained the milk and butter. In the meantime he tried to get the American Hospital on the telephone. An ambulance arrived, but only after much precious time had been lost.

Ollie lived for one week, and that one week according to the doctors, she owed to Jack's quick thinking in giving her the warm water, milk, and melted butter. But it was a week of agony for the poor darling . . . . She fought a hopeless battle, dying, finally in my brother's arms.

Is this account reliable? Mary Pickford was always fiercely protective of her brother and other family members. Her account reads a bit like a movie script, and a large portion of blame is conveniently laid at the feet of an unnamed maid. If Olive really thought the pills were aspirin, why did she swallow so many of them—most of the bottle, and all in the dark?

Was this really an accident, as police documents say? Or was it suicide by a distraught young woman who had had too much to drink?

Some newspaper accounts say Olive swallowed the pills. Others said she first dissolved them in alcohol, which in fact was the way those pills were supposed to be prepared. But how could she have done that "accidentally"?

Was it murder by a guilty husband who had also had too much to drink and had his eye on someone new? Perhaps. It would fit Jack's playboy persona. But Jack and Olive did seem to have a powerful love match, whatever anyone else thought.

One of the few things we know for sure is that Jack and his former brother-in-law Owen Moore stayed by Olive's side at the American Hospital in the Paris suburb of Neuilly-sur-Seine, watching her endure the effects of the caustic overdose, until she died on September 10, 1920. She was twenty-five years old.

No one knows what Olive's dying thought was, but no one could blame her if it was a memory of the glamour and delight of standing on the New Amsterdam stage, soaking up the adulation of the *Follies* audience far across the sea.

Olive's funeral was held September 29, 1920, at St. Thomas Episcopal Church in New York, which still stands on Fifth Avenue at 53rd Street. Some fifteen thousand people packed the streets around the church. A fistfight erupted at the door among fans trying to get inside to pay their respects.

Also in attendance were all three of the filmmaking Selznick brothers, one of whom served as a pallbearer. The Selznicks saw to it that Olive's coffin was transported in a special ivory-inlaid limousine.

She was buried at Woodlawn Cemetery in the Bronx, where you can still sometimes see flowers left by her headstone which reads only "Pickford." More than a hundred years after her death she still has fans.

Olive was scarcely settled in her grave when Hollywood began capitalizing on her notoriety. On October 4, the studio released her final film, *Everybody's Sweetheart*, which was advertised as "The final appearance before the camera of America's captivating screen star, whose loss of life in the whirl of the shameless orgies of Paris, has aroused the world to the dangers of the sinful city."

In addition to its general release, the film was treated to a special showing at Broadway's Lyric Theatre, across 42nd Street from the New

Amsterdam. When the box office jumped for *Everybody's Sweetheart*, Olive's earlier films got special rereleases as well.

EARLY SIGHTINGS

Not long after the hoopla began to die down, stagehands at the New Amsterdam began telling friends that they had run into Olive backstage. Impossible, they were told. Olive is dead. But no, they said, it was Olive, all right. She was even wearing her white *Follies* dress, her beaded headpiece, and her sash. The only odd thing about the girl they saw was what she was carrying: a big blue bottle—the same type of bottle that had held Jack Pickford's syphilis medication.

Moreover, the mysteriously familiar-looking woman would sometimes speak. "Hiya doin', fella?" was her standard greeting. People from different shows and different walks of life who didn't know each other—but who had witnessed one of Olive's appearances—would imitate her voice for the author of this book, and always imitated it the same way.

And then, for many years from the 1930s to the 1980s, sightings seem to have ceased, or went unreported. These were dark years for the New Amsterdam Theatre, and 42nd Street as a whole. Once the Acropolis of American theatre, the block between Broadway and Eighth Avenue declined into the Necropolis. One by one the great Broadway theatres of the street—the Selwyn, the Victory, the Harris, the Liberty, the Times Square, the Apollo, the Lyric and more—switched from legitimate theatre to movies. The movies went from first-run, to B movies, to violent exploitation films. And then, in some cases, to pornography. Hookers and drug dealers could be seen gathering under the New Amsterdam's marquee when the weather turned ugly.

To its credit the New Am never sank to showing porn, though it did screen films for a long time. The main stage and the Roof theatre, where Olive made her debut, were sometimes used by Broadway productions for rehearsal space. Director Moss Hart famously coached Julie Andrews there for her role as Eliza Doolittle in *My Fair Lady* (1956), and Tommy Tune (with help from Thommie Walsh) created some of his Tony Award–winning choreography there for *The Will Rogers Follies*.

During its time as a movie theatre, Olive still materialized occasionally. In a 1997 letter to the *New York Times*, a writer named George Strum recalled just such an encounter and expressed concern that the renovations, then in progress, might drive her away: "There appeared in the balcony late at night to cleaning ladies, janitors, projectionists, or patrons as a beautiful woman in a white gown carrying a blue bottle. Thomas died of an overdose of medication probably kept in such a bottle. Perhaps the racket of constructions scared her ghost away. Maybe she is waiting until the hoopla quiets down to reappear, or maybe she has reappeared, though people now think she's a wayward hooker or a homeless person."

The New Amsterdam changed hands several times during its long, dark period. It was bought by the Nederlander Organization, which had announced plans for a refurbishment that never came about. In 1992 the 42nd Street Development Project bought the theatre to preserve it, engaged Hardy Holzman Pfeiffer Associates to restore it, and began to seek a partner to run it.

It was at this point that Walt Disney CEO Michael Eisner took his now-famous walking tour of the onetime "House Beautiful" and saw the building's potential as a Broadway home for Disney Theatricals, a new branch of the company devoted to creating projects for the legitimate stage.

Disney spent $36 million on its refurbishment, added to a $26 million loan from the 42nd Street Development Project. As chronicled in Mary C. Henderson's authoritative book, *The New Amsterdam: The Biography of a Broadway Theatre*, architect Hugh Hardy oversaw the work, which took five years. From the audience's point of view, the centerpiece was the detailed restoration of Herts & Tallant's gorgeous art nouveau trimmings and decorations inside the auditorium, complete with plaster and terra cotta swirling vines, ripe fruit, leaves and sprites, all done in green and peach tones.

The rest of the building was brought up to date, too. One sad loss was the New Amsterdam Roof Theatre on the top floor, which could not be brought up to fire code because the only escapes were via elevator and a narrow staircase. The proscenium of the Rooftop was kept, as was the raised glass promenade where girls would dance and sashay while the audience below could get a peek at their ankles, et cetera.

The stage where Olive once did her dances was portioned out into offices, including the throne room of Disney Theatricals president Thomas Schumacher, now the nerve center of Disney's theatre empire in New York. The trap door was sealed off and the trap space became a storage room. More on that later. The theatre reopened in 1997 with *King David* and *The Lion King*, the latter of which won the Tony Award as Best Musical that year, as was still going strong in 2022, as this book went to press.

But what about Olive?

A phone rang in the bedroom of Dana Amendola, the man whom the Disney corporation had put in charge of its latest acquisition, the derelict New Amsterdam Theatre. Amendola squinted at the clock. Who could be calling at 2:30 a.m.? He picked up the phone. It was the security guard he'd hired to patrol the New Amsterdam. The man was hysterical. During his rounds of the theatre, he was crossing the stage when his flashlight picked up a beautiful young woman who had absolutely no business being there at that hour. She had a flowing white dress and was holding a blue bottle. He shouted at her and she left the stage—by walking right through the wall on the 41st Street side.

The watchman wanted to resign on the spot.

Amendola, who is still in charge of the New Amsterdam as vice president of operations, had heard the stories of the ghostly *Follies* girl.

Workers who renovated the theatre for its 1997 reopening reported numerous encounters with Olive. She appears almost exclusively to men, and often acts flirtatiously.

A master woodworker called my fellow *Playbill* writer Louis Botto in 1996. The worker was part of the team refurbishing the upper balcony of the New Amsterdam and had an unusual story. It seems he had discovered that Disney had bought more than a building. It also bought the ghost of Olive Thomas.

He was working alone, carefully installing a custom-lathed molding, when gradually he became aware of the sensation that he was being watched. He looked up, and there, sitting just a few feet away, was a beautiful young woman.

"Hi, fella!" she chirped, in a high-pitched Betty Boop accent.

The man squinted. She wasn't dressed for a work site. She was wearing an old-fashioned drop-waisted white dress and her hair was strangely bobbed. Her eyes were bright, but the skin of her cheeks was a fish-belly white. She was holding a blue bottle.

Thinking she was a girlfriend of one of his coworkers who had wandered off, his first instinct was to scold her. "This is a construction site. You shouldn't be up here without a hard hat!"

She opened her mouth to laugh at him, but no sound came out.

The woodworker got up and brushed off his hands. He called over his shoulder, "Who let this lady up here?"

There was no answer. And when he turned back, the strange girl was gone. When he went down to complain to the foreman, the foreman and his assistant looked at each other oddly. The foreman took the woodworker aside and, after asking for a description of the girl, explained, "That was Olive."

As Olive's host, Dana Amendola has become something of an authority on her life. He said she is a regular visitor to the theatre—appearing, or making her presence known—mainly after audiences depart.

She's generally benign but can be temperamental.

Two portraits of her now hang backstage, and everyone employed there makes a habit of saying "Good morning, Olive!" when they arrive for work, and "Good night, Olive," when they leave. As long as they do so, Olive seems appeased. If they forget, things around the theatre have a way of going a bit wrong: props go missing, actors stumble, and mysterious static is heard on the sound system.

As a visitor to the New Amsterdam, you can see her lobby portrait easily. The theatre has its main entrance and distinctive marquee on West 42nd Street, reading horizontally in tiny italic type "*NEW*," then plunging four stories vertically, in block capitals, "AMSTERDAM." The theatre space itself actually backs up on West 41st Street. To get in through the front entrance on 42nd, audiences must enter beneath this dramatic signage and promenade down a long gallery lined with portraits of the great stars who graced the stage back in the age of Zieg-feld: Fanny Brice, W. C. Fields, Eddie Cantor, Marilyn Miller, Ziegfeld himself, and others. But the last portrait on the right is a stranger—though she did star on the theatre's stage. It's our friend, Olive Thomas, looking angelic.

There is another portrait of Olive on the 41st Street side of the the-atre, but visible only to those who enter the stage door. A smaller image of Olive hangs there, to greet and be greeted, as the actors, stagehands, musicians, and other stage artists come to work each day, so full of life.

Amendola became not exactly a believer—but certainly less of a skeptic—when he was touring the site of the old New Amsterdam Roof Theatre in the mid 2000s. The space was being converted to offices. As he passed below the stage, he suddenly and distinctly heard the sound of tap-dancing on the boards above him. Climbing quickly to stage level, he found he was alone.

Olive often appears in the space beneath what was once the stage of the New Amsterdam Roof Theatre, the space where Amendola heard the mysterious tap dancing. The space is now used for storage, but employees report seeing a woman there, or sometimes a disembodied part of feet climbing a staircase.

During previews of the 2011 musical *Aladdin*, Amendola said a female replacement conductor, who had worked on *Mary Poppins* at the New Amsterdam and knew about Olive, was getting ready in a dressing room. Reading from an email from the conductor, Amendola said she spoke out loud to Olive, "Well, Olive, I'm back again, and I'm a little nervous. I just wanted to introduce myself again and ask if you could please give me some good luck." Then she mused aloud, "I won-der what the *Follies* girls would have thought of a female conductor?"

And just then, according to the conductor's email, four of the round dressing room bulbs flickered on and off for a few seconds and then stopped. The bulbs were all new, having just been replaced for the new show. "It was like a wink. She was signaling that she was fine with the idea."

Thomas may have made another appearance in the middle of the crowded New Amsterdam orchestra section. In 2014, during the run of *Aladdin*, an audience member came up to one of the ushers during a performance and asked if she could have a booster seat for her child. The usher said, "We don't like to interrupt a show, so we waited until the intermission and came to her with a booster. But we found she already had one. When we asked where she had gotten it, she said a 'lady at the back of the theatre' had gestured to where they were. Now, we don't have a woman at the back of the house who does that in the middle of a show. We checked and none of the staff had done it. So, you can take that how you like, but it was kind of freaky."

Amendola said that if there really are such things as ghosts, and if the New Amsterdam is indeed haunted by one, he's happy about it. "We embrace it. She's never violent, always playful. She kind of embodies what we're all about here at Disney. We're in the business of happiness, and to have someone from so long ago acknowledging that she's pleased makes us feel like we're doing the right things."

However, Amendola said Olive is unpredictable and doesn't "perform" on cue. "She doesn't appear on Halloween, for instance. When people try to find her, they can't. She tends to appear just at the moment we forget about her—when we're busy putting in a new show or putting a new office in. When there are changes happening."

"You don't find Olive," he added. "She finds you."

There is one other time when Olive has displayed pique: when people from her era came to visit. The latter rarely happens anymore because there are so few still alive from that time, but it happened fairly regularly when Broadway Cares/Equity Fights AIDS began inviting surviving *Follies* performers to its annual "Easter Bonnet" competition there in the 1990s and into the first years of the new century.

Olive seemed to have a special problem with one of the star attractions of "Easter Bonnet": Doris Eaton Travis. Born in 1904, Travis grew up in vaudeville as part of a sibling act, the Seven Little Eatons. Travis made her Broadway debut in 1917 as the youngest-ever dancer hired for the *Follies*, and appeared in the 1918, 1919, and 1920 editions of the revue, plus the 1919 *Midnight Frolic*. Like Olive, she went on to appear in silent films and returned to the stage when she could. She later retired from the stage, became a dance instructor at the Arthur Murray Studios for a time, and helped her husband manage their horse ranch. In 1997 she returned to New York, along with several other surviving *Follies* alumnae, to help Disney celebrate the reopening of the New Amsterdam.

At age ninety-four, Travis was invited to appear as a special guest at the 1998 edition of "Easter Bonnet." Eaton, who was still spry and still able to dance, taught the young performers the steps to her dance specialty, "Ballin' the Jack," and led them in a sample performance. Travis repeated this performance each year until she was 105. And then, when she was 106 in 2010, made her final appearance riding on a specially designed vehicle onto the New Amsterdam stage. She died a month after that appearance, listed in obituaries as the last surviving *Follies* girl.

Interviewed by the author of this book, Travis did not have kind words to say about Olive, whom she felt was a prima donna.

The feeling appears to have been mutual.

According the Amendola, one year when Travis appeared on the New Amsterdam stage, the large set for then-tenant *The Lion King* started to shake violently with no apparent cause. Another year, all the light bulbs on one of the office floors burned out simultaneously without any detectable problem with the electrical system.

Whenever Travis set foot in the building, trouble started—though it seemed to cease once the "Easter Bonnet" performances got underway.

Olive can still manage a ghostly scare when she wants to. A doorman at the New Amsterdam said that on the previous summer a recently hired nighttime security guard was crossing the stage when he ran into the figure of a woman clad in old-fashioned clothes, and carrying a blue bottle. As happened before, when the guard confronted her and asked what she was doing there, she reportedly turned and walked through the wall.

More than a century after her death, Olive remains one of the best-known of all the Ziegfeld Girls, the subject of films, books, and at least a half dozen websites.

And that has created a problem for the staff at the New Amsterdam. Amendola said they get asked about Olive all the time, which is not a problem. But many of Olive's craziest fans have tried concealing themselves in corners of the theatre, hoping to stay after it is closes, so they can catch a glimpse of the glamorous ghost. Amendola said his staff now does a special sweep of the theatre each night to catch stowaways and escort them out.

Olive is still queen of the New Amsterdam and still patrols her domain. During the Disney renovations of the 1990s she was spotted in the upstairs space that once housed the New Amsterdam Roof.

She was walking through the air, unsupported. Research shows that the Roof once sported a notorious glass-bottomed promenade above the audience, designed so swells could peek up women's skirts, and naughty flappers could tease them with their frillies. When the space was renovated as offices for producer Disney Theatricals, architects made sure to restore part of the glass promenade in memory of the space's scarlet past.

The New Amsterdam Roof Theatre may be long gone, but Olive still sometimes puts on a show for the boys.

Amendola has become a keeper of the Olive Thomas flame. Among other things, he clocks reports of her appearances. Not a few of them show that Olive still has a temper. He recalled, "In 2013 a creative development team—a man and two women—was in one of the offices in the old New Amsterdam Roof. They were talking about the film *The Artist*, which was set in the silent film era. They were wondering how many *Follies* girls became film stars, and they mentioned that Olive Thomas was one, but Mary Pickford was the REAL star of the silent era. Now, maybe Olive got a little upset about that because when someone said, 'I wonder what Olive Thomas would think of *The Artist*,' a stack of DVDs on the table next to them flew into the air and crashed across the room. They all sat in stunned silence. That stack had been there for a long time and there was no obvious way they could have fallen, let alone flown across the room."

Reports of her appearances rolled in over the years. Actor Josh Tower, appearing in *The Lion King* in 2004, said "Olive Thomas, is very active. Stuff happens all the time. Things disappear and no one can find them. Some nights everything goes wrong, like there are gremlins in the works. We just say, 'Olive is at play.'"

A "live" Olive Thomas returned to the stage one more time in 2015 with the opening of an immersive theatre experience called *Speakeasy Dollhouse: Ziegfeld's Midnight Frolic*, presented in the shell of the Liberty Theatre, just a few doors west of the New Amsterdam on 42nd Street. Audiences were invited to wander through the backstage area, equipped with a popular bar, while they watch the story of Olive's life and death enacted over and over, along with what were described as scenes inspired by her Ziegfeld show of one hundred years earlier. These were performed on the Liberty Theatre stage by actors playing the likes of Eddie Cantor, Josephine Baker, and Olive (Syrie Moskowitz) herself.

In the show, playwright/director Cynthia von Buhler didn't take a stand on how she believed Olive died. Each time her death was repeated, it was shown a little differently, like an old-time cliffhanger film serial. Sometimes it was suicide, sometimes an accident, sometimes a murder by her husband. Of course, your author *had* to see this, and I found it fascinating. But the play didn't offer a lot of explanation, and if you didn't know Olive's sad story, you might have been confused by the play. Still, you would have had to wonder if Olive's ghost might have floated down the street to see it one night, and what she thought about it.

Seeing that show was part of my hobby. I have been collecting ghost stories and visiting haunted theatres for more than a quarter century. Although I have met many people who have had personal experiences with the supernatural, I personally have had only one. And it was with Olive Thomas—or, more accurately, Olive under a different name.

I was working at *Playbill*, hosting a radio show that played on the now-defunct PlaybillRadio.com. My sign-off was the cheery, "From the heart . . . of Broadway." Halloween was approaching and instead of doing a standard celebrity interview, I wanted to go out into the field and, if I could, interview an actual ghost.

Hey, why not? It was worth a shot.

I picked Olive, since she was the most active ghost on Broadway. I asked permission from Amendola to spend the night inside the New Amsterdam with my microphone and recorder. He said he'd try to get permission, but Disney said no. Insurance liability, blah, blah, blah. Fine. I respect that. However, I was granted permission to stay inside the theatre late into the evening with Amendola as chaperone, and I was welcome to set up my recorder and leave it running all night.

The sound recorder was set up on a laptop in an office located where the old *Midnight Frolic* stage used to be. The next morning, I played back the recording and found I had picked up some odd scrapes and thumps at about 3 a.m. But they could have been anything, really. No voice. No "Hiya doin', fella."

I expressed my disappointment, especially since I now had nothing for my radio show. Amendola asked if I wanted to interview one of the staffers who had encountered Olive—and more than once.

Now this was more like it!

I was introduced to a bearded stage carpenter, a salt-of-Manhattan backstage Broadway veteran who had seen it all and was not prone to nonsense. He told me that Olive appears in many spots around the New Amsterdam building, but most frequently in what used to be the "trap" room beneath the stage of the New Amsterdam Roof Theatre. In active theatres, the trap is used to house props or pieces of scenery, and sometimes machinery to make stage turntables turn. Special effects are sometimes prepared there, and lifted onto the stage through small doors, familiar to the world as "trap doors." Actors make surprise entrances and exits through them. Olive made her *Midnight Frolic* entrance onto the stage through the door from this very trap.

Now that the New Amsterdam Roof stage area is used for offices, the door has been sealed and the old trap space is used for storage.

The carpenter took me inside this storage room. It was appropriately dark and spooky. Light from the access hallway spilled through the door and illuminated some hulking old set pieces, including a large door attached to a heavy metal doorframe that leaned against one wall. It must have weighed eight hundred pounds. He and I were the only ones in the room.

I called out, "Olive? Olive Thomas?" a few times.

Nothing happened.

The carpenter told me that Olive materializes when she wishes and will not be summoned or ordered around. He told me that she had sometimes appeared to him and others as a pair of disembodied feet and calves in high heels clattering up a flight of stairs. I laughed at the thought of it and told him of my experiences interviewing one of Olive's last contemporaries, Doris Eaton Travis, mentioned earlier. I recounted how miffed she had been when I called her "Doris," and how she preferred to be addressed as "Mrs. Travis."

That gave me an idea. I knew that women of that era, especially actresses, liked to be addressed by their married names. So I called out, "Hello, Mrs. Pickford!"

And that's when the eight-hundred-pound doorframe went "clunk."

The carpenter and I both laughed at that. We assumed it was a coincidental clunk and nothing supernatural. Just a funny trick of timing.

But then my guide said it was just the sort of thing Olive would do. She liked moving things around. We examined the piece. It was a steel door with a doorknob, attached by normal hinges to the massive steel frame. It was designed to be lifted into place by a forklift or toe jack and attached to the wall and floor, perhaps of a stage set. The top leaned against the wall of the trap, slanting down to where it rested firmly on the floor. My companion said he wasn't sure what had made it go "clunk."

I decided to try again. "Mrs. Pickford, are you there? It's me, Robert Viagas, from *Playbill*."

And in the half-light of the trap, the big frame seemed to shift upward a quarter inch or so, and clunk down again.

I quickly checked my recorder. Yes! I had gotten the sound—what there was of it—on tape.

Further shout-outs to the ghost went unheeded and unclunked. I had just barely enough audio to make a broadcast out of it, what with the interview and my narrative—though the two clunks themselves scarcely made compelling radio.

Still, it's my story. And it's what I tell people at my ghost talks when asked if I have ever had a ghostly encounter of my own. The only photographic evidence I have obtained are a few snaps of the runway in the Disney offices that show some of what the ghost hunters call "ghost orbs," but which could be just the reflection of light on the lens.

So, I am left to wonder: What did Olive—Mrs. Pickford, I mean—think of me? Was she trying to signal me? Was she trying to say, "Yes, I am here!" Or "Please leave me alone"? Was she trying to drop the door on us? After all, she does have a history of temper and mayhem. Or was it just a lucky coincidence, the heavy door taking that particular moment to shift and settle a little bit? But then again, it happened twice, and only when I called her by her married name.

Whatever it was, I suspect there is yet no end to the escapades of Broadway's sexiest and busiest spirit. I hope I get to meet her again.

Postscript: Olive is not the only ghost at the New Amsterdam. Backstage workers tell of an entity that consists only of a disembodied shadow. This shadow is most often seen sliding up and down the steps in the building's stairway. They have given it a name that has become my favorite theatre ghost moniker: "The Black Goon."

2

THE PALACE THEATRE

Broadway's Palace Theatre at Seventh Avenue and 47th Street is said to have more than one hundred and twenty ghosts, including those of both Judy Garland and Harry Houdini. It's the most extensively haunted theatre in America, and very possibly the most haunted single building anywhere.

The theatre has since been refurbished twice, with a third—and most ambitious—renovation in the works as this volume goes to press. It now functions as a standard Broadway house, mainly for musicals like *La Cage aux Folles*, *Beauty and the Beast*, and *Aida*, all of which enjoyed long runs there.

But in its heyday in the 1920s, the Palace was the pinnacle of the vaudeville world. "Playing the Palace" was a byword for reaching the top of their crazy profession. The flagship of the B.F. Keith chain of theatres was the place all acts dreamed of performing. Some acts worked decades honing fifteen minutes of "A material," a killer bit of shtick that would land them on that stage at last.

Small wonder, then, that once performers made it there, not even death could get some of them to leave.

The vaudeville industry was unofficially but emphatically divided into Big Time, Medium Time, and Small Time, denoting the status of the booking. Small Time vaudeville acts played the smallest theatres in smaller towns, for smaller pay, naturally. They generally were required to play more performances per day as well, as many as five daily, from late morning to late evening.

Acts with proven drawing power could play larger theatres in bigger cities for better pay, and could also command better position on the "bill." Second to last of the ten or so acts at each performance was considered the prime spot. The worst acts, dubbed "cleanup acts," were relegated to the final spot. They were so bad that theatre owners would book them to drive the audience out of the theatre so it could be cleaned and made ready for the next show.

The best of the best acts were the "Big Time" acts, which commanded top pay, billing, and programming spot in the biggest cities. Big Time acts were booked by the Big Time "circuits" (i.e., chains) of theatres, like the Orpheum Circuit and B.F. Keith's Circuit. The latter was managed for many years by Edward Franklin Albee, adoptive father of Edward Albee, who became one of America's greatest playwrights.

And perched atop this pyramid was the best booking in the vaudeville world, "playing the Palace," B.F. Keith's Palace Theatre in Times Square, New York. Among the stars who played the Palace were the Marx Brothers, Fanny Brice, Fred and Adele Astaire, Ethel Waters, Houdini, Eddie Cantor, Will Rogers, Bert Williams, Helen Keller, Ed Wynn, and Buck and Bubbles.

Would-be Palace headliners sometimes took rooms in the boarding houses that lined the block of West 47th Street between Sixth and Seventh Avenues, near the Palace stage door. The block became known as

"Dream Street" and the stretch of sidewalk on Times Square in front of the Palace's main entrance became known as "The Beach" because acts would wash up there, performing their shtick and hoping to impress someone coming or going through that door to land a booking.

Once an act had been designated Small Time or Medium Time, it was very difficult to move up. Even among Big Timers, getting to play the Palace was often a lifelong dream and the result of a lifetime of hard work. As you may imagine, many performers who reached that pinnacle never wanted to leave. Even after death their souls found a way back to its hallowed precincts.

The Palace opened on March 24, 1913, the brainchild of Martin Beck, who was at the nucleus of the raucous world of vaudeville booking. (More on him in chapter 4.) Vaudeville was just coming into its full power. He built his Palace into the biggest of Big Time during and after World War I. However legendary the theatre became, its golden age lasted less than twenty years. In 1927 a movie called *The Jazz Singer* opened just a few blocks uptown, ushering in the era of talking pictures. The picture starred Al Jolson, one of the many stars who had sung on the Palace stage. Vaudeville was doomed, helped along by the fact that people could see, and now hear, many of the same stars at a cinema for a fraction of the cost of live theatre—especially as the Great Depression broke over the country and the world.

Despite its beauty and legendary aura, the Palace struggled to survive for the next three decades, sometimes even showing films (but never porn). Among the high spots of the 1950s was Judy Garland's landmark concert shows. More on that later in this chapter.

In 1965, the growing Nederlander Organization took ownership of the Palace and refurbished it as a legitimate Broadway theatre, opening with Bob Fosse and Gwen Verdon's *Sweet Charity*, and continuing with *Applause, Woman of the Year, La Cage aux Folles*, and *The Will Rogers Follies*—all Tony Award–winning Best Musicals.

Concessionaires like Ray Venezia, who worked for Disney at the Palace from 2000 to 2003 during the run of *Beauty and the Beast* and is now a professional photographer, had to stay behind to count the money, put it in the safe, and log the paperwork. Late one night, between 11 p.m. and midnight, Venezia was sitting in his office off the long, wide promenade leading from Times Square into the recesses of the legendary playhouse.

Out of the corner of his eye, Venezia saw someone flash by the open door of his office, momentarily blocking the light filtering in from the hall behind it. Venezia looked up just in time to see a man in a long coat and a hat stride past the doorway. No one else was supposed to be in that part of the theatre at that hour. And it was odd that anyone would fail to stop and say hello.

Venezia jumped up and stuck his head out of the doorway. The long lobby was empty. He called out, but there was no answer. He had just gotten settled down again when in his full view, the man flashed by again. There was an odd look in his eye. It never even flickered on him. The gaze was concentrated straight ahead.

This time, Venezia jumped up too fast for anyone to have gone more than a few steps up the promenade. But again, there was no one there. Venezia immediately picked up the phone and called the stage doorman at the other end of the building to ask who, if anyone had gotten permission to be prowling around the theatre at that hour. The doorman asked for a description, and then laughed.

"That's just the ghost."

When Venezia asked for an explanation, he was directed to house manager Dixon Rosario, who filled him in on enough ghosts to fill a separate Who's Who in the *Playbill*. Some are visible human figures, some are rags of mist, some are balls of light, and some just leave you with sensations of cold or odd feelings of dread. These appear mainly to theatre staffers in the honeycomb of passageways and offices underneath and above the performing space, most of which are just storage areas now. People who work there after dark say the theatre is always filled with the sounds of knocking and disembodied footsteps. One area of particular activity is the original box office, which once fronted on 47th Street, and which is now used for storage. The theatre has chronic trouble keeping its ghost light lit.

And over the next few years, Venezia had a chance to meet—or at least observe—several of these phantasms personally.

One night, he walked up the darkened, heavily carpeted stairs to the mezzanine. As he rose, he heard it: a child's dimly echoing laughter, footsteps running back and forth, and an odd, muffled rolling noise.

He rose to the level of the back of the mezzanine and as he rounded the corner from the top of the stairs, he got a clear view of the wide aisle that runs along the back of the seating area.

There was a little boy, dressed in the style of a newsboy of the 1910s. He was playing, as he always does, with a toy truck, rolling it back and forth and making motor noises. He looked like any other child playing with a toy, except that he was long dead.

When he saw Venezia, he looked up, made eye contact, and fled in fright. About halfway down the passage, he seemed to be swallowed into an unknown place. He simply went out, like a light, and his toy vanished with him.

And he has a playmate, though they're never seen together. If you scan the seats of the rear mezzanine, your eye may suddenly light on the curly head of a hollow-eyed little girl who stares emptily at you, then slowly sinks out of sight behind the seat backs. When you go up to find her, the little girl isn't there.

It must be sad for these spirits, having to play in this dark place forever. Yes, there are warm and happy people who come and sit among them every night, and that must be a comfort, but their warmth is always just out of reach.

There's one ghost at the Palace who has a rich and creepy story—though it seems to be one of those stories that has grown with the telling and may have more than a little fiction mixed in.

Here is the legend, as Venezia heard it, and as it has been handed down among theatre folk: Louis Borsalino was a vaudeville tight-rope walker who is said to have fallen to his death on the stage. Unlucky visitors to the Palace have occasionally seen a tight rope stretched from the box seats at house left to the edge of the mezzanine, house right. "Stagehands say that when the theatre is empty, Borsalino's ghost can be seen swinging from the rafters. He lets out a blood-curdling scream, then reenacts his nose dive."

Those who have reported seeing Borsalino's act are also said to have met untimely ends themselves shortly thereafter. The dead acrobat is a harbinger of death. That's the legend.

Now let's look at the actual record. Borsalino's name was reported that way in the *New York Times* and the Associated Press, but there is no record of a performer of that name booked at the Palace. However, there are published reports that an acrobat named Louis Bossalina, a member of a high-flying gymnastic act called the Four Casting Pearls, fell during a performance on August 27, 1935. The team was performing a signature stunt forbiddingly called "The Death Loop," and Bossalina was injured, but not fatally.

According to Frank DiLella of Broadway Up Close Walking Tours, Bossalina "would grab the hands of his partner (who was hanging by his legs from a trapeze) and then Bossalina would be launched into the air, do two somersaults, and then grab his partner's hands again on the way down."

But on the day in question, things went wrong; as Bossalina was launched into the air, his hands slipped. "As the half-full theatre of eight hundred watched in horror, Bossalina flew into the wings and plummeted eighteen feet to the stage floor. He was taken to the nearby Flowers Hospital on Fifth Avenue, with a fractured pelvis and internal bleeding."

Bossalina survived and, after a lifetime of performing, died in 1963 in Reading, Pennsylvania, at the age of sixty-one.

So should his haunting be crossed off our list? Not so fast. As we know from the stories of Olive Thomas and others, you don't have to die in a place in order to haunt it.

In the late 1960s, DiLella reports, "stagehands repeatedly noticed a figure in white swinging in the air above them; then the figure would vanish and they would hear a blood-curdling scream. The first few sightings of this white-costumed figure prompted research, and the stagehands unearthed what appears to be the only photo of the Four Casting Pearls—wearing white unitards."

So apparently Bossalina didn't die at the Palace. But it seems that he is spending the afterlife reenacting his terrible fall—perhaps as a warning.

JUDY GARLAND

Sweet-faced actor Jack Haley, a longtime Broadway and vaudeville performer best known for playing the Tin Man in the landmark 1939 film *The Wizard of Oz*, wrote about the Palace, "The walk through the iron gate on 47th Street through the courtyard to the stage door, was the cum laude walk to a show business diploma. A feeling of ecstasy came with the knowledge that this was the Palace, the epitome of the more than 15,000 Vaudeville theatres in America, and the realization that you have been selected to play it. Of all the thousands upon thousands of Vaudeville performers in the business, you are there. This was a dream fulfilled; this was the pinnacle of Variety success."

But there may be an even more famous ghost lurking in the crimson, gold, and marble of the Palace—Haley's *Wizard of Oz* costar, Judy Garland.

Actor Ryan VanDenBoom, who has been seen on Broadway in *MJ The Musical*, *Something Rotten*, and *Bandstand*, told the Ghosts and Murders blog that when he was appearing at the Palace in the 2011 revival of *Annie*, he heard a disembodied voice calling "Judy" when he was alone in his dressing room.

If you stand in the center aisle of the orchestra with your back to the stage, you'll see, in the center of the wall at the top of the aisle, a door. This was installed during the 1950s at the behest of La Garland who played three legendary sold-out concert runs at the Palace, in 1951, 1956, and just before her death from a drug overdose in 1967. It was her habit to end each performance by striding into the audience, up the main aisle where her legions of fans strained to touch her outstretched hands, and then vanish through this door, which was dubbed the Judy Garland Exit.

36

Venezia and his fellow Palace workers say they never pass this door without the overwhelming feeling of a presence that causes the hair on the back of their necks to stand on end. "It's like you're being watched; like someone is waiting for you to say or do something," he said.

And so they do. Each employee has their own greeting ritual as they pass the door. Venezia, who usually passes it on his way out of the theatre late at night, just says "Good night, Judy." And the feeling evaporates.

Actress Orfeh was featured in the 2007 musical *Legally Blonde* at the Palace. She said, "When things get wacky at the theatre we say, 'Oh, Judy is angry.' Things tend to happen in a cluster on one [performance]. Things get stuck, things get lost. How could it be happening? It's either Judy or the gremlins having fun."

Sarah Solie, who appeared there in the 2012 revival of *Annie*, said, "Some people reported faucets turning on by themselves and I think our original PSM [production stage manager], Peter Lawrence, had a sighting in the balcony."

Why would Garland, who died far away, haunt the Palace? Venezia said, "It could be that these people have come back to what was their greatest success, and where they felt their greatest love."

HOUDINI

Master magician and escape artist Harry Houdini (born 1874; died 1926—on Halloween) is also said to haunt the Palace.

Houdini was, for a time, the highest-paid act in vaudeville. No pull-a-rabbit-out-of-a-hat clichés for him. His illusions included swallowing a pile of sewing needles and a length of thread, then, after pausing for a refreshing drink of water, pulling the whole parade of needles, perfectly threaded together out of his mouth.

But his specialty was using his immense physical strength, his expertise at picking locks, and a powerful ability to control his entire body including his lungs, in a series of "impossible" escapes. For example, to prove he wasn't using stage tricks in his escapes, he had himself strapped into a straitjacket, then hung upside-down from a building, in full view of the public, freeing himself and climbing down in under three minutes. He made even better time when his hands and feet were chained and he was nailed into a wooden packing crate loaded with two hundred pounds of lead and dropped into New York City's East River. He escaped in under a minute.

However Houdini is still best remembered for his Chinese Water Torture Cell, in which the handcuffed magician was lowered, upside-down into a locked, water-filled, glass-walled container from which he had to escape before he drowned.

At the Palace, his ghost has sometimes been seen upside-down, struggling through this act, just as he did in life.

Of course, there are nearly a dozen other places that claim a Houdini ghost too, including an estate in Hollywood (where he once lived); Montreal (where he died); a pool in Hollywood (where he swam); The Houdini Magical Hall of Fame in Niagara Falls, Canada; three different locations in Detroit (where he was embalmed); and even elsewhere in New York City: McSorley's Old Ale House in Greenwich Village. Where he supposedly appears in the form of a cat.

That's all ridiculous, of course. To be in that many places at one time you'd have to be a . . .

LIFTING THE PALACE

And, with the current (as of spring 2022) renovation, these and all the other ghosts of the Palace are finding themselves just a little bit closer to heaven.

Working under the joint title TSX Broadway, a consortium of developers (Maefield Development, L&L Holding Company, and Fortress) is performing unprecedented surgery on the venerable old playhouse. The supremely ambitious $2.5 billion project, which has been underway since 2019, involves jacking up the century-plus-old Palace from its current location on the ground floor and raising it to the third floor of a massive new complex that will surround it with retail below and a hotel above.

Although the interior performing space is landmarked and cannot be changed, the Palace will boost its seating from the current 1,743 seats to about 2,200, which will make it the biggest theatre on Broadway (a title previously held by the 1,933-seat Gershwin Theatre on 50th Street).

What effect this may have on the many resident revenants remains for the theatregoers and theatre workers of the mid-2020s and beyond to discover.

3

THE BELASCO THEATRE

Broadway's Belasco Theatre is named after its ghost. The ghost built the theatre.

David Belasco (1853–1931) was part of the great nineteenth-century tradition of theatre owners/producers/playwrights. They did it all, jacks of many trades. Belasco built the current New York theatre that bears his name in 1907, but only after decades as a successful author of dozens of passionate melodramas, two of which achieved immortality as source material for Giacomo Puccini's operas *Madama Butterfly* and *La Fanciulla del West* (*Girl of the Golden West*).

Belasco loved theatre so much, he spent nearly every waking hour at the theatre, writing, managing, or directing his plays. He also spent every sleeping hour there, since he made his home in a specially built ten-room duplex apartment above the stage and auditorium in his West 44th Street theatre. At the end of each day, Belasco would finish counting the box office, extinguish the house lights, then begin his homeward commute . . . up the stairs.

Belasco devoted so much of his life to the building, it's no surprise that he seems to be spending his afterlife there, too.

Broadway's Belasco Theatre. The two short towers on either end and the pointed section of the façade with the round window contain the haunted Belasco apartment. Photo by Robert Viagas

He's one of the most solid theatre ghosts. No wispy ectoplasm for him. He appears much as he did later in life: tall, with tousled white hair and wearing the cassock and clerical collar that was his lifelong affectation. He was known, during his life, as "The Bishop of Broadway." Those who have glimpsed him, but don't know his story, nevertheless have nicknamed his ghost "The Monk"—though, as late *Playbill* historian Louis Botto has pointed out, there was nothing monk-like about his lifestyle. Many a pretty young actress furthered her career by accompanying the old lecher up to his apartment via a phone-booth-sized private elevator.

The *New York Times* reported that Belasco was "an avid collector of pornographic objets d'art," which he displayed in niches in the apartment. He also built peepholes so he could view actresses in their dressing rooms. The paper said a group of British actors who ventured into the apartment with flashlights long after Belasco's death, were greeted with a stench that turned out to be from a dead pigeon.

In keeping with Belasco's obsession with things medieval, his apartment was designed to look like a monastery: heavy dark wood, vaulted ceilings, and large, multipaned windows. A dramatic staircase leads to an even higher room, which was Belasco's boudoir.

This brings us to his well-bounced casting couch. Today he would be branded as a serial abuser, but in his own time the practice was paternalistically considered acceptable if not honorable. But no sense sugar-coating it: Belasco may not have been quite a Hollywood mogul of some more recent examples, but he was on the same continuum. He had that private elevator installed to whisk "ambitious" and attractive young actresses up to his apartment for private "auditions" and coaching sessions.

He may have dressed like a clergyman, but he did not practice celibacy.

Shortly after his death on May 14, 1931, at age seventy-seven (not in his theatrical apartment, but at the nearby Hotel Gladstone), Belasco's ghost began to show himself. Actors stepping out on the stage unawares would suddenly notice a lone, dark figure sitting in the balcony, watching them intently. This ghost had a voice, too. He would sometimes walk right up to actors and shake their hands, telling them that they had done a fine job at a performance. More than one actress filed complaints with the house manager that an old man dressed up like a priest had pinched her bottom. The uninitiated were often terrified by these encounters. Veteran actors looked forward to them (though not necessarily the pinches), seeing them as good omens.

Belasco manifests himself in other ways, too. The reek of cigar smoke has permeated more than one production in which no one smoked, and long after smoking was banned in the theatre. Closed doors on the set have been seen to magically open in unison as the curtain rises.

There is another synchronized door story as well. One usher said that as she was closing up in the lobby one night at the Belasco, the house manager playfully called out, "Good night, Mr. Belasco." And, even though the exterior doors were pulled shut and there was no wind, all the outer lobby doors swung open silently and in unison. She said she asked to be transferred after that and still won't work at the Belasco.

His frequent appearances on dark stairways or hallways have sent a chill up more than one spine. In a story about the Belasco phenomenon, the *New York Times* reported that a caretaker's dog would growl at an unseen intruder every afternoon at precisely 4 p.m., when, apparently, the theatre's namesake would make his rounds.

Longtime theatre columnist Earl Wilson reported in 1975 in the *New York Post* that the ghost would "scream blood-curdlingly through the night" when the theatre had a show he didn't like.

Technically, Belasco's new landlord was the woman who took over as house manager of the theatre in the 2000s. When you walk in the main entrance to the Belasco you see the ticket windows directly in front of you. Beautifully carved in dark wood, the same as in the apartment above, they are Belasco originals that have been restored. Above the ticket windows you see a series of distinctive rondel glass panels. Behind these glass panels is the house manager's office where she works. If you go up the stairs from the first floor and enter her office she will tell you that the ceiling of her office lies directly beneath the floor of the legendary Belasco apartment. She took the job having heard the Belasco legend but not thinking much of it.

Shortly after she began working in that office, especially after hours when the theatre was empty, she began hearing footsteps upstairs, presumably in the apartment. Thinking that a trespasser might have broken into the building, she went out into the hall, climbed the stairs to the top floor of the building, and opened the door into the apartment. It was dark and dusty and empty. She called out and searched the apartment but could not find anyone or anything amiss.

In the weeks and months to come, she started noticing more odd things. She could sometimes hear 1920s-style music coming through the ceiling, and then the sound of a crowd chattering, clinking glasses, and sometimes even dancing to the music. She would again climb the stairs, again open the apartment, and again find it empty—and silent. It happened enough that she had a motion sensor and a camera installed in the apartment that fed into her desktop computer. When she would start to hear the music and the talking and the dancing she would open up her computer and check the feed. The motion sensor was detecting nothing and the camera showing only an empty apartment.

Earlier in this chapter it was mentioned that Belasco had a special private elevator built for his homeward commute and to facilitate his sexual escapades. The elevator, which did not meet New York City building and fire codes, had been sealed off many years earlier. That's why it seemed strange when the house manager started getting complaints from audience members and from employees that the elevator was sometimes heard to rise and descend during performances and at other times. Its motor could be heard starting up and the car could be heard rising and descending in the shaft, like someone was using it. The manager assumed there was an electrical malfunction and wanted to avoid a fire hazard, so she ordered the motor and the car to be removed and the shaft resealed.

When workers from the Shubert Organization opened the shaft, they found to their surprise that the motor and the car had been removed long before, and the shaft was . . . empty. So what was making the sound that everyone was hearing? In addition to a ghost manager and ghost partyers it appears that the Belasco Theatre also has a ghost elevator.

Nothing stops Belasco from holding court in the theatre that bears his name. But there was one incident that seems to have slowed him down. In February 1971, a long-running production of *Oh! Calcutta!* transferred to the Belasco from the Eden Theatre, where it had been playing for a year and a half. Kenneth Tynan's revue featured skits by the likes of Samuel Beckett, Jules Feiffer, John Lennon, Leonard Melfi, David Newman, Robert Benton, and Sam Shepard. Nearly all dealt with sex in various ways, and the show became notorious for its frequent displays of nudity.

It's hard to imagine the philandering Bishop of Broadway as having a prudish side, but according to people who worked at the theatre during the show's eighteen-month run there, Belasco's ghost seemed to take a sabbatical. For years afterward his appearances were rare, and it took a long time before he was back to his usual schedule.

Possibly his standards (his public ones, anyway) were offended in some way. But he departed or withdrew for more than twenty years—until a 2001 revival of *Follies* apparently revived Belasco as well. The story of aging alumni of the fictional *Weissman Follies* who confront ghosts of their younger selves, *Follies* may be the ultimate theatrical ghost story. Ghosts haunt the 1971 Stephen Sondheim–James Goldman musical—ghosts of vanished youth, ghosts of roads not taken, ghosts of love lost—but their memories are never quite buried. *Follies* is the story of a reunion of performers in a Ziegfeld-like revue at the crumbling theatre where they once performed—a theatre set to be demolished. As the now middle-aged and elderly characters make their entrances, they are joined by the beautiful ghosts of their younger selves, which only the audience can see. The two main couples, Buddy and Sally, Ben and Phyllis, come for a pleasant evening of nostalgia, but find themselves drawn into recollections of the terrible romantic mistakes—their "follies"—made when they were young, and haunting their unhappy lives ever since. Spending your life with the wrong partner is a special kind of hell. The ghosts fear that hell but are too damned by their foolish mistakes to go to heaven, so they are left to relive their personal follies (along with the glittering *Follies*) as they wait for the wrecker's ball.

For the pure number of glamorous fictional ghosts on stage, it's hard to beat *Follies*. Perhaps the show hit home for the spirit of the Belasco's namesake. He seems to have resumed his appearances, though not quite as busily as before.

THE LADY IN BLUE

There is one report of Belasco's malevolence. The ghost is said to have pushed a young actress down a flight of stairs, killing her, and thereby gaining himself some supernatural company. I could find no concrete records of such a death, though several people who have worked at the theatre said they swear by it. They feel certain there is a second ghost at the Belasco, a female ghost of melancholy—and sometimes angry—mien. They call her the Woman in Blue or the Blue Lady.

This ghost manifests as a blue cloud or mist, one that feels bitterly ice cold to anyone who touches it. Actress Rose Perez, who made her Broadway debut at the Belasco in 2003, reported encountering the mysterious blue mist, and feeling chilled to the bone as she passed through it.

Star Judith Ivey tells of noticing someone watching her during a supposedly closed rehearsal. She had heard the story of Belasco's ghost, but naturally took it with a grain of salt and didn't even think of it when she saw the strange man in the mezzanine. She complained to the director, Matthew Warchus, who shouted to the man, who was he and what was his business? The man rose silently and departed up the aisle and out the back.

An assistant was sent to collar the interloper, but he never found anyone. The stage doorman said no one was in the theatre who was not on the sign-in list. It gradually dawned on them all that they'd had the privilege of meeting the legend for themselves.

During the run of *Passing Strange* in 2008, Daniel Breaker told *Playbill* in an interview that one evening he was putting on his makeup in his dressing room mirror when he saw an old man with white hair sitting behind him, silently watching him. When Breaker turned around to demand what he was doing there, the man, who resembled nobody working on the show, was gone. Breaker reported the incident to the house manager, and was told, "You just saw David Belasco."

Dominic Brewer, who appeared in *Twelfth Night* and *Richard III*, wrote, "We've not spotted Mr. Belasco or any of the theatre's reported spooks to date, but with the white make-up several of the cast wear for *Twelfth Night*, along with the eerie gliding of the female characters, you'd be forgiven for thinking you'd spotted a ghost backstage. However, we have had a strange happening onstage: one evening the candles on one of our six hanging candelabras completely burnt down, probably twice as quickly as all the others, without any perceptible draft or obvious external influence. An unsolved mystery."

Belasco house manager Stephanie Wallis said that Belasco has been comparatively quiet in the years since the 2010 renovation. To tease him out, the creators of *Hedwig and the Angry Inch* actually wrote Belasco into the script. Each night, Neil Patrick Harris and his successors asked if anyone in Box B had seen the ghost, but there were no takers. Nevertheless, Wallis said, "I can tell you that the front door of my office suspiciously locks itself from time to time—and I know it isn't me doing it."

Belasco's apartment is still there, though a 2009–2010 renovation of the theatre did not include the apartment—which could easily become a museum or, if the Shuberts want to make a steady income from the building, a luxury apartment that could rent for millions.

Actors who have appeared at the theatre are mainly fascinated by the building's ghosts. Several have obtained permission to explore the apartment including expeditions from *Hamlet* (1996) and *Dracula, The Musical*. Despite some serious amateur ghost hunting, they reported nothing but cobwebs and clutter in the abandoned space . . . along with a distinctly eerie feeling.

Among the very few non-employees the Shubert Organization has allowed to visit the Belasco Apartment is the author of this book. I was working at *Playbill* at the time (2010) and decided to do a video story about the renovations to the Belasco Theatre that had just been completed.

Accompanied by the renovation project manager, Thomas Stein, and the Shubert vice president–facilities, John Darby, I got to see, close up, the painstaking renovation of the theatre's woodwork and especially the unusual stained glass settings for the theatre's house lights. I asked how they were able to reach to clean them and change lightbulbs, and they showed me how maintenance people accessed them, not from the auditorium, but from small hatches hidden in the floor of the apartment above.

The apartment is all any person with a monastic obsession—and a fat budget—could ask for. It was Belasco's personal sacristy, with heavy carved-wood fittings, cathedral-glass windows, gothic-arch doorways, and a few remaining bits of furniture that could have been used as an ambo that you might see in a church sanctuary. Behind a sturdy door was a heavy safe that resembled a tabernacle. Most of the furniture had been removed and there were loose wires hanging from the ceiling. I was warned off a spot in the floor and a flight of stairs up to the boudoir, which I was told had some rot and might not hold my weight. (You can see my tour on YouTube: www.youtube.com/watch?v=iXLXBqtApw4&t=309s.)

The atmosphere in the apartment, apart from being sweltering on a hot summer day, was not terrifying or ghostly—though I might have gotten more of that if I had gone after dark instead of on a bright afternoon. Still, in the milky light filtering through the windows, there was a clear sense of being in the personal space of one of Broadway's great mad geniuses. He had made his eccentric life work for him. Maybe he was watching us that day. Eighty years after his death, he was still very much of a "presence" there.

David Belasco apparently wasn't ready to give up his life in the theatre when he gave up his life, as the stories of ghostly parties in the apartment bear witness. He appears to be alive (sort of) and well in the twenty-first century, continuing his run as Broadway's most extroverted ghost.

4

THE AL HIRSCHFELD THEATRE
AND THE ST. JAMES THEATRE

RENAMING THE MARTIN BECK THEATRE

Martin Beck is one of the newest of Broadway's ghosts, or, at any rate, the most recent to manifest itself.

Broadway's Al Hirschfeld Theatre was better known to generations of theatregoers as the Martin Beck Theatre, many of whom weren't happy to learn that it was going to be renamed in 2003, even if it was for the beloved theatrical caricaturist and *New York Times* regular, Al Hirschfeld.

Apparently one of those who objected the most was Martin Beck himself.

Beck (1868–1940) was one of the formative personalities in the world of vaudeville. As a master booking agent, the Hungarian-born immigrant was instrumental in creating the national organization of theatres known as the Orpheum Circuit. One of the greatest attractions of the Orpheum Circuit was master magician Harry Houdini, whose ghost was discussed in chapter 2. Houdini is said to haunt the Palace Theatre, which is appropriate since he was one of the acts Beck booked there. But Beck did not only book the Palace's acts, he was also instrumental in building the theatre.

Through his booking policies, Beck made the Orpheum Circuit the Promised Land of vaudeville and the Palace its crown jewel, the theatre that every act wanted to play, and every fan wanted to see.

It was shocking, therefore, in 1923, when the other principals of the Orpheum company ousted the powerful Beck in what has been described as a "boardroom coup."

Though deeply wounded, Beck decided to fight back. He bought land on the theatrically untouched west side of Eighth Avenue, two blocks from the Palace, and built his own rival theatre, which he named after himself. It would be very satisfying to say that the Beck was a bigger success than the Palace, but it wasn't. Unable to book the very acts he had boosted to stardom, he went to work for Orpheum's rival, Keith-Albee. By the time Keith-Albee merged with Orpheum during the Great Depression to form Keith-Orpheum, vaudeville was dying. A further merger created the film company Radio Keith Orpheum (RKO), and Beck managed the theatre that carried his name until he died.

Like the Palace, the Beck was repurposed as a Broadway house. Audiences have been unfazed by its supposedly unfavorable location on the "far" side of Eighth Avenue—actually just a couple of hundred feet from the Golden Theatre on the "near" side. The Beck housed more than its share of hits, including the original *Bye Bye Birdie*, *Into the Woods*, *Kinky Boots*, and *Moulin Rouge!*

All was well there for decades. No sign of any supernatural activity. But then came 2003.

Current owners, the Jujamcyn Organization, announced in 2002 that they would rename the theatre for Al Hirschfeld, who had been creating his distinctive black-and-white drawings of shows since the 1920s—images that always contained his daughter's name, "NINA," worked into the lines.

Broadway traditionalists were not happy at the erasing of Beck's historical name. But it must be said that Hirschfeld was certainly worthy of having a theatre named after him. Drawn from the comfort of a special barber chair he kept at his home, his sketches were regularly featured in the *New York Times* and had come to have a close association with Broadway. Many actors felt they hadn't "made it" until they had been drawn by Hirschfeld. Several shows used his caricatures as their poster image, including *My Fair Lady*.

It seems that a group of theatre fans and historians had launched a campaign to rename some of the Times Square area theatres that had neutral names or were named for those whose connection with Broadway had been largely forgotten. They wanted the theatres renamed to honor prominent theatre personalities. That's how the 46th Street Theatre became the Richard Rodgers, the Uris became the Gershwin, and the Virginia became the August Wilson.

Hirschfeld seemed like a natural. Seemed.

As the renaming date approached, Martin Beck's moniker was removed from the marquee, and replaced with Hirschfeld's. But that wasn't all. In addition to his name, the new owners decided to festoon the sign with one of Hirschfeld's own drawings—a self-portrait—rendered in neon lights. Not a bad idea at all, considering it was the first theatre to be named after a graphic artist like Hirschfeld. His classic drawings could become a permanent part of the Broadway scene. Fine.

However the self-portrait they chose was one of Hirschfeld using his own head as an inkwell. His head seems to have been carved open to show that the inside was full of a red substance obviously supposed to be ink. On the page it was a cute, if macabre, idea. Rendered in neon light looming over the sidewalk, it looked like Hirschfeld was trepanning himself. After some comment, the red ink was later changed to blue, and, in its most recent transformation, only the drop of ink hanging off the pen is in blue.

Hirschfeld didn't have long to enjoy the honor. Within weeks of the name change announcement, Hirschfeld was dead, just shy of his one-hundredth birthday. The renaming went ahead anyway in June 2003.

Strange things began happening around the theatre almost immediately. Actors working there in the show *Wonderful Town* (2003–2005) reported that almost immediately upon their arrival in fall 2003, things began to go oddly. One actress combing her hair said she was suddenly struck violently from behind by a small figurine she kept in her dressing room. When she turned, however, she found she was completely alone. But that wasn't all. Props and personal items would vanish from one place, only to be found in a strange and unlikely different place. Anyplace the theatre's new logo appeared, it was often stained, or things would be found lying beneath it, as if thrown.

Worst of all, that neon "Al Hirschfeld" sign on the marquee constantly malfunctioned. Electricians at the theatre found they couldn't keep the sign lit long. There was always some inexplicable glitch.

To the actors, however, there was no glitch. They were sure the PO'd poltergeist was Beck himself, signaling his displeasure at his theatre's rechristening.

Playbill historian Louis Botto wrote, "The cast was disturbed by a ghost who caused havoc onstage during performances [of *Wonderful Town*]. It was concluded that the specter was none other than a very irritated Mr. Beck, unhappy that his theatre had been renamed."

The problems eventually stopped—after Jujamcyn unveiled a prominent plaque in the lobby acknowledging Beck and listing his accomplishments. Things have mostly been quiet at the Hirschfeld since then. Perhaps Beck, a master negotiator, realized this was the best deal he was going to get, and took it.

However, it doesn't seem like he's been completely mollified. According to one report, as shows come to the end of their run, "jeers appear to be heard from nowhere."

Although it is very likely that he persists somewhere inside the old playhouse, one of Broadway's most distinguished and beautiful, happily watching ticket holders line up for the theatre's current hit, the Tony Award–winning Best Musical, *Moulin Rouge!*

THE LAUGHING GHOST OF THE ST. JAMES

Theatre ghosts usually follow an unwritten code: no manifestations while the curtain is up. But there is one notable exception on Broadway: the laughing ghost of the St. James Theatre.

Standing on West 44th Street, just steps from Eighth Avenue (and just around the corner from the Hirschfeld), the St. James has a distinguished history going back nearly a century. Originally built by and named for Abraham Erlanger, one of the principals of the dreaded Syndicate booking agency of the period, the theatre became one of the most eagerly sought after in the Times Square area. Among its megahits

Broadway's St. James Theatre. Photo by Robert Viagas

were the original productions of *Oklahoma!*, *The King and I*, *Hello, Dolly!*, *The Pajama Game*, *Barnum*, *My One and Only*, *The Producers*, and plenty more. It is now owned by Jujamcyn Theatres.

Recently home to Disney's *Frozen* and David Byrne's *American Utopia*, the theatre houses a ghost who bursts out in insane laughter at inappropriate moments during performances. The laughter has persisted two or three times a month, through at least two decades of shows.

Two ushers interviewed for this book say that the laughter sometimes gets so bad that audience members complain, thinking it's just an unruly fellow audience member. But pinning down the location of the alleged laugher is like trying to reach the end of a rainbow: you can never get to it. People in the orchestra section complain, "Can you please ask that person in the balcony to stop disrupting the show?"

Meanwhile the upstairs ushers are getting a similar grilling: "Can you please ask that person down in the orchestra to stop disrupting the show?" They don't realize they are lodging complaints against Broadway's most unmannerly ghost.

Among the most prominent sufferers from the snickering spirit was Laura Benanti who gave her Tony Award-winning performance as Gypsy Rose Lee in *Gypsy* there in 2008. The ghost interrupted her performance of the quiet, emotional solo "Little Lamb." The song is sung by Louise (future stripper star Gypsy Rose Lee), a young woman, and a secondary member of her domineering mother's vaudeville troupe of "youngsters." Although the "kids" are technically too old for their parts, Louise's mother lies about their ages to the booking agents.

At one point they throw a birthday party for Louise. Afterward, when she's alone, she sings a tender song to her stuffed animals about her unhappiness. At the climax of the song, she reveals the truth: her mother has never told her how old she actually is.

It was at this crucial moment in the pin-drop-quiet theatre, that the Laughing Ghost burst out in completely inappropriate hysterics, ruining the heartbreaking moment.

Benanti told the author of this book that the first time she heard the laughing she assumed it was a drunk, but when it occurred several times in the same spot, she was mystified until the legend of the ghost was shared with her.

The origin of this demented shade is completely unknown. "I doubt it's a professional," sniffed one of the ushers. "A pro would never disrupt a performance like that."

Speaking of professionals, you might stop and wonder why the world theatre is so filled with people who swear by ghosts and faithfully practice superstitions. No whistling backstage! No saying the real name of the Scottish Play! And so on.

For all their confidence on stage, many in the theatre business live in a perpetual state of insecurity. Am I good? Why didn't they laugh tonight? What if the reviews are bad? What if the producer decides he hates me? How do I pay for my sublet if the show closes?

Some shows run for years and provide the closest thing to job security that actors and stagehands ever know. More often, however, their jobs last only a few weeks—days. Imagine having to find a new job every couple of months. Imagine not being able to find one for a long time.

Even those who stay with the theatre when the shows change—the box office personnel, the people who maintain the theatre and keep it clean—can be sensitive to the supernatural. Long after the audience leaves a theatre for the night, there are still things to be done. The floors are swept, wigs are combed out and stowed away, rigging is secured and the sets left ready for tomorrow's curtain. These are people who spend hours alone in the theatres, with the lights turned down. Their imaginations, or just their sensitivities, have a lot of time to play.

That's perhaps why theatre folk seem to live so close to death. Even their terminology involves death. If they do badly, they "die" on stage. If they do really well, they're "killing 'em." If you forget your lines or break character by laughing, you're "corpsing."

A lot of theatre superstitions are designed to ward off desperately feared disaster or bring desperately needed good luck. You'll notice that a lot of theatre workers develop friendly relationships with the theatre ghosts—the souls of people who have finally escaped the cycle of hit and flop and are able to stay at one show forever. Heaven! (Or the next best thing.) Seeing such ghosts is often taken as an omen of success, of a good show, of rave reviews. These ghosts' imprimaturs are sought and cherished.

5

OTHER BROADWAY GHOSTS

The previous chapters deal with the best-known and most active ghosts on Broadway, but there are plenty more.

THE BROOKS ATKINSON THEATRE

Longtime *New York Times* critic Brooks Atkinson (1894–1984) was considered by many to be the very model of a modern, evenhanded, and literate theatre critic. His ghost is said to haunt the theatre that bears his name at 256 West 47th Street. Originally the Mansfield, the theatre was renamed for the reviewer in 1960. With about 1,100 seats, it is suitable for large plays or small musicals, and in recent years housed hits including *Peter and the Starcatcher*, *Waitress*, and *Six*.

The dapper, bespectacled, and mustachioed ghost is sometimes spotted sitting in the orchestra in the "*Times* seats"—center section on the aisle in rows E or F—sometimes puffing on a pipe. Actor Lee Wilkoff, who appeared at the theatre in the drama *Democracy*, said another actor on the production spotted Atkinson's distinctive form siting in the audience, apparently taking notes for a review, at the first preview in 2004.

The legend may have inspired the cast of the long-running musical *Rock of Ages* to stage a series of short films in the style of a horror movie. Collectively titled *The Haunting of the Brooks Atkinson Theatre*, they were shot in 2009 in the spooky hallways and basement of the Atkinson. The *ROA* cast teams up with friends from the then-running *Spring Awakening* to track down the murderous sickle-bearing "ghost," only to fall victim to it, one by one. A clip can be viewed on YouTube: www. youtube.com/watch?v=orGProT9pLE.

THE WALTER KERR THEATRE

The Walter Kerr Theatre on West 48th Street—another theatre named for a critic—may also be haunted by its namesake, the respected longtime reviewer for the *New York Herald Tribune* and then the *New York Times*. Actor, playwright, and director Ruben Santiago Hudson, who was appearing there in August Wilson's drama *Gem of the Ocean* (2004), said, "I sometimes feel a cold breeze go by, even when no door is open. I mentioned it to my dresser and he said, 'That's the ghost of Walter Kerr!'"

RADIO CITY MUSIC HALL

Radio City Music Hall is believed to host the well-dressed shade of its builder, Samuel L. "Roxy" Rothafel. Born in Germany, he was brought to the United States as a child toward the end of the nineteenth century. He came of age during the golden years of vaudeville, but quickly latched onto movies as the wave of the future. He managed various legitimate theatres and movie houses in New York City, where he

Broadway's Walter Kerr Theatre. Photo by Robert Viagas

developed his concept that movie theatres should be palaces, designed to sweep audiences into an opulent fantasy world as compelling as the movies they were going to see there.

The philosophy was embodied in his first great custom-built movie house, the eponymous Roxy Theatre at 153 West 50th Street between Sixth and Seventh Avenues, which cost a then-astronomical $12 million. The 5,920-seat theatre opened March 11, 1927, and became known for its mixture of movies and lavish stage shows, and for its platoon of impeccably dressed male ushers. Songwriter Cole Porter memorialized them in his song "You're the Top," a comic list of sublime people, places, and things, including "the steppes of Russia" which he rhymed with "the pants on a Roxy usher."

But the Roxy wasn't enough for Rothafel. He planned to top the Roxy with his even gaudier and more splendid theatre around the corner, the art deco masterpiece Radio City Music Hall, which opened in 1932. Its attractions included a precision-dancing corps originally dubbed the Roxyettes, later shortened to the Rockettes (partly as a salute to Rockefeller Center, of which Radio City is a part).

The Roxy was torn down in 1960. A photo of movie star Gloria Swanson standing amid the ruins was said to be an inspiration for the Stephen Sondheim–James Goldman musical *Follies*. But Radio City Music Hall still stands today as a monument to Roxy's vision. The Musical Hall building even included an apartment that became Rothafel's home.

Roxy always reserved a seat in Row D for himself and a companion, and it is this seat that he is said to haunt. Rothafel died in 1936 only a few years after the music hall opened. Ushers at the theatre have reported finding his seat down at the end of the night when all of the others are up. There have also been reports of ghost-like activity in his well-appointed private apartment, which is still maintained. Guided tours of the theatre include a stop in this apartment.

L'Aura Hladik, author of "Ghosthunting New York City," said she interviewed Dr. Philip Schoenberg, founder and head tour guide for Ghosts of New York Walking Tours, who reported that Roxy has been seen at the theatre "on opening nights . . . accompanied by a glamorous female companion." Roxy's ghost, along with the beautiful lady on his arm, "has been seen walking down the aisle toward their seats, vanishing before reaching them."

THE EUGENE O'NEILL THEATRE

The Eugene O'Neill Theatre lacks the cachet of famous theatres like the Palace and Winter Garden, and doesn't enjoy a reputation as a haunted "house" like a Belasco or a New Amsterdam. But this medium-size theatre playhouse has had some interesting manifestations in the last quarter century, some involving well-known Broadway personalities.

Built in 1925 at 230 West 49th Street as the Forrest Theatre, it was renamed in 1959 after our only four-time winner of the Pulitzer Prize for Drama, including *A Long Day's Journey into Night.* Is it he who haunts the theatre that bears his name? Maybe. Hard to tell. The spirits of the O'Neill don't materialize, so we can't recognize them. They are closer to poltergeists in that they move things and sometimes even touch people, but don't show their faces.

Donna Lynne Champlin, appearing there with Patti LuPone, Michael Cerveris, and Merwin Foard in *Sweeney Todd* in 2006, reported, "We believe there are at least two ghosts at the Eugene O'Neill [home

Broadway's Eugene O'Neill Theatre. Photo by Robert Viagas

of *The Book of Mormon* from 2011 into the 2020s], one male and one female. During previews, things would randomly fall from the upstage prop shelf—sometimes dangerous things like gardening shears—when no one was remotely near it. Actors' hair gets tugged every once in a while, and they have heard their characters' names whispered in their ears onstage."

Champlin, who played Pirelli the barber in the innovative production of the cannibalism-themed musical, continued, "There is a strong smell of lilac sometimes, downstage left. My whistle disappeared from my bloody lab coat pocket (which never leaves the stage) and was found down in the basement in the 'Dead' rack of clothes." Turn to chapter 6 for Champlin's ghost story involving Patti LuPone at the O'Neill.

And it was not just Champlin who noticed the phenomenon. Merwyn Foard, a standby in that production, said, "I set up the cot to take a nap between rehearsal and a show and asked out loud for a wake-up call. Sure enough, at 6:30, I was awakened by a slap on the bottom of my shoes that almost sent my head crashing up into the bottom of the counter that I had placed my cot under. No one was in the room but me!"

It doesn't sound like the way O'Neill comported himself in life—which, he wrote, was "for each man a solitary cell whose walls are mirrors." But big life events, like death, will probably change a guy. Then again, not all theatre ghosts had to have been stars.

THE LYCEUM THEATRE

Like his contemporary David Belasco, Daniel Frohman was one of the theatre people who produced, directed, often wrote, and sometimes starred in their own shows. Furthermore, like Belasco, Frohman lived in his own special roost above the theatre he owned.

Sailing home from shopping for shows in 1912, Frohman was booked aboard the maiden voyage of the luxury liner *Titanic*. (See the full story of Frohman and his beloved Empire Theatre in chapter 12.)

His onetime apartment now houses the Shubert Archive, an immense collection of paper records, photographs, contracts, clippings, artwork, and anything else you might want to know about the Shubert Organization's operations over the past century. Frohman has been reported greeting rare visitors at its door like it was still his home.

If you visit there, you can see a tiny Hobbit-size doorway on the north wall of the apartment. Open it, and you get an eagle-POV view

Broadway's Lyceum Theatre. Photo by Robert Viagas

of the Lyceum stage, from high above the top of the balcony. Froman had this door built so he could monitor rehearsals and performances, according to writer Louis Botto. He was especially concerned with the acting of his wife, Margaret Illington. "If his actress wife was overacting, he would wave a handkerchief to suggest she tone it down."

The door is also visible from the house if you go down the house-right orchestra aisle to the edge of the stage and crane your neck up to the ceiling over the top balcony.

The Lyceum Theatre, which opened on November 2, 1903, at 149 W. 45th Street is the oldest continually operating theatre on Broadway. Only the New Amsterdam is older—by a single week—but it was closed for many years.

Coleman Domingo, who played Mr. Bones in the 2010 musical *The Scottsboro Boys*, said the cast sensed the spirits in the Lyceum: "We didn't see any, but we could feel them. On the Friday night of our last weekend, things were happening backstage and onstage with the lights and the computer equipment. We definitely felt we were in the presence of some ghosts."

Bob Fosse, one of the greatest director-choreographers ever to work on Broadway and who developed a sinuous, sexy hip-bumping style, directed shows in many Broadway theatres—but never the Lyceum. So why is it that people who work there believe he haunts the theatre's balcony? We will touch on this theatre again in chapter 12.

But inside the audience space, the sound of footsteps and the distinctive smell of cigarette smoke (in a no-smoking building) has led people to believe it might be Fosse, still chain-smoking the cigarettes that helped usher him into an early grave at age sixty. These manifestations were felt most strongly when Chita Rivera, who costarred in the original production of Fosse's *Chicago*, starred there in the 2016 musical *The Visit*. Theatre workers have also been known to find hats similar to the ones Fosse wore to hide his thinning hair. No one claims them.

Rivera's costar on that show, the late Roger Rees, who also worked with Fosse, told the *New York Post*, "Bob Fosse told me he loved going to the back of the balcony to look at the stage from the top of the theatre." This may explain his manifestation in the Lyceum's cheap seats.

As we saw in the chapter on the Belasco Theatre (with more to come), the smell of tobacco smoke is often a harbinger of the ghostly experience. That may decline in the years to come as fewer people smoke. If the ghosts vaped, will anyone know?

THE IMPERIAL THEATRE

Though the Imperial Theatre, with its entrance on West 45th Street but it's audience space on 46th, is traditionally believed to be haunted by *prima donna* Ethel Merman, she hasn't been seen recently. Instead, the young ballerinas of *Billy Elliot* were convinced that the theatre's girls' dressing room was haunted by a spirit they named Fred. Ballet girl Kara Oates reported seeing a bathroom door open and close by itself while she was doing homework there in 2011.

It's not the theatre where Merman starred most frequently. That distinction belongs to the Neil Simon Theatre (formerly the Alvin) on 52nd Street. But Merman starred in some of her biggest hits at the Imperial: *Annie Get Your Gun*, *Call Me Madam*, and, after having opened elsewhere, Merman moved there during the run of *Gypsy*.

She may have been supplanted by a more recent ghost: Tony Award–winning costume designer Martin Pakledinaz, who died in 2012 while his second-to-last show, *Nice Work If You Can Get It*, was running at the Imperial. On July 12 of that year, just days after Pakledinaz had died of brain cancer, the show's stars, Matthew Broderick and Kelli O'Hara, found themselves with a quandary. The Imperial stage was littered with beads used to adorn costumes. The beads were a problem because they were a hazard to anyone trying to perform Kathleen Marshall's 1920's-inspired choreography on the stage. The beads were so obviously a problem that both stars ad-libbed about them in an attempt to explain their presence. But that only confused the audience, so Broderick took a moment after curtain calls later that evening to explain their interpolated comments about the beads.

There were two curious facts about these particular beads. One was that none of the stagehands had any idea where they had come from. They probably just fell off someone's costume, right? The problem is, none of the costumes in the show used that kind of bead. Broderick explained this to the audience and said the company had concluded that the beads were Pakledinaz's unique way of "making his presence known one last time." Broderick then led a moment of silence for the lost designer.

THE BOOTH THEATRE

The Booth Theatre on West 45th Street across from the Imperial is mentioned in chapter 8 in the section on President Abraham Lincoln's assassination, which occurred famously at Ford's Theatre in Washington, DC, during a run of *Our American Cousin*. Lincoln was shot to death by John Wilkes Booth, part of the famous Booth acting family. As handsome as John Wilkes was reported to be, he had nowhere near the critical acclaim of his brother, master actor Edwin Booth (1833–1893). So lasting was Edwin's reputation that the theatre bearing his name wasn't built until 1913. He was remembered with deep respect.

Edwin knew nothing of his brother's plan to kill the president, and afterward Edwin considered giving up the stage out of shame for John Wilkes's action. But his fans supported him and (mostly) didn't blame him, though the killing will always be a stain on the name of Booth.

Despite its age, the Booth Theatre has no reported ghost stories—but it does have a Ghost Light story. During the 2013 revival of Tennessee Williams's *The Glass Menagerie* with Cherry Jones, Zachary Quinto, and Celie Keenan-Bolger, set designer Bob Crowley had the Wingfield family apartment seeming to float in the midst of a pool of black liquid. Carrying the Ghost Light and its pole up through the center of the trap was an unusual chore, so house electrician Susan Bennett-Goulet took the unusual step of suspending the Ghost Light above the stage. She warned the stagehands and others to be careful crossing the stage when the light was lit but, sure enough, a security guard missed the memo and fell into the black water one night.

Don't worry: He survived and did not become a ghost. But he came close.

One more item about the Booth Theatre: the very last Broadway production of *Our American Cousin* opened on November 29, 1915, starring E. H. Sothern. That's fifty years after the assassination.

Guess which theatre it was booked into?

THE STEPHEN SONDHEIM THEATRE

Chapter 5 described Martin Beck, the annoyed ghost of the Hirschfeld Theatre. Beck built the theatre and slapped his own name on it, and so it stayed for much of the twentieth century. Apparently he wasn't happy when they renamed his theatre in 2003, and he came back from the afterlife to let everybody know.

But there's another irritated original namesake on Broadway—and this one had his named carved into the front of the theatre: old-time manager Henry Miller. The "front" is significant because it was the only part of the theatre to have gotten a Landmark designation. New owners of the site effectively demolished the old Henry Miller's Theatre (the only namesake theatre with a possessive attached to the name—to emphasize ownership), but spent a small fortune to preserve the landmarked

The marquee and landmarked façade of Broadway's Stephen Sondheim Theatre. Photo by Robert Viagas

brick facade during the rebuilding in 2008–2009. The new theatre on the site—which uses the preserved façade as its own—was designed by architect COOKFOX from the ground up as Broadway's first fully "green" theatre. To help defray expenses, the new operators offered to rename the theatre for a generous donor and the donors asked in 2010 to name it for Stephen Sondheim as a gift for their friend's eightieth birthday.

Sondheim, who died the day after Thanksgiving 2021, is considered by many to have been the greatest theatre composer-lyricist of the late twentieth century. His musicals include *Sweeney Todd*, *Company*, *A Little Night Music*, *Into the Woods*, and plenty more. Early in his career he wrote the lyrics for *West Side Story* and *Gypsy*. If you don't know who Sondheim is, you probably shouldn't be reading this book.

Anyway, many readers of this book would also probably consider the renaming of the Miller as the Sondheim something of a step up, but Miller's ghost apparently didn't see it that way, even though the architects saluted Miller by taking the old sign that once hung on the marquee and installing it at the stage door, visible from a public alleyway through a large glass window.

Kevin Duda, who played Neil Sedaka in *Beautiful: The Carole King Musical* at the Sondheim in 2014, wrote about a strange experience there: "I . . . had stayed late one night at the theatre, walked up to the stage door, and realized that I had forgotten something in my dressing room. I noticed the old 'Henry Miller' sign, which hangs over our security desk at the stage door, as I return to the elevator to go downstairs. I murmured, under my breath, 'Wow, I wonder what Henry Miller thinks of his sign being relegated to the stage door?' And the elevator bounced. And stopped. I was stuck. I screamed for about five minutes and finally, Adolf, our head of security, came to my rescue and pried the doors open. I have NEVER said Henry Miller's name in this theatre again."

THE GERSHWIN THEATRE

Another newish Broadway house that is already accruing ghosts is the 1971-vintage Gershwin Theatre, perhaps stimulated by its long possession by *Wicked*, a musical about the rivalry and friendship between two witches. Cast member Michael McCorry Rose said in 2013, "According to sources in the know about these things, we have three ghosts. Drew (a.k.a. Dennis) is the only one we know by name. The other two

The marquee and entrance to Broadway's Gershwin Theatre. Photo by
Robert Viagas

ghosts who are regularly seen haven't been named, but one dresses in a nineteenth-century blue suit and the other wears a white T-shirt."

In 2012 another *Wicked* cast member, Jonathan Warren, reported, "Nathan Peck got tapped on the shoulder before his front-of-house monkey flight one evening. When he turned around, no one was standing near him. Later, when he told people about it, Kevin Hucke mentioned that he had the same experience throughout the years in the same location. It is rumored and believed to be the ghost at the Gershwin."

THE RICHARD RODGERS THEATRE

The owners of what is now the Richard Rodgers Theatre had a much easier time of it than the owners of the Hirschfeld or Sondheim. The theatre was built in 1925 as Chanin's 46th Street Theatre, later shortened to just 46th Street Theatre—a perfectly descriptive name, but one that lacked poetry—and lacked a troublesome former namesake.

Renamed in 1990 for another master composer, Richard Rodgers, the theatre has the distinction of having housed more Tony Award–winning Best Plays and Best Musicals than any other theatre: eleven, including *Guys and Dolls* (1951), *Damn Yankees* (1956), *How to Succeed in Business without Really Trying* (1962), *1776* (1969), *Nine* (1982), and *Fences* (1987).

This theatre deserves to be haunted, and so it is.

Blanca Camacho, a swing and understudy in the original cast of Lin-Manuel Miranda's *In the Heights*, wrote in *The Playbill Broadway Yearbook 2009–2010*,

Broadway's Richard Rodgers Theatre. Photo by Robert Viagas

I was almost embarrassed to poll *Heights* folk with this question as I was certain I would get blank stares or quizzical looks—I'd never heard such rumors [of ghosts] at our theatre UNTIL I ASKED! The house staff had plenty [of] stories to share. There are reappearing red lipstick smudges in the ladies' room. They get painted and wiped, but inevitably returned. Stall doors open by themselves. Dressing rooms have strange sounds, and things spontaneously fall off shelves in one of them. After-hours brings bizarre howling sounds, chandeliers moving, the sound of people talking. Jimmy, our doorman, armed himself with a baseball bat one such evening. Guess he was going to take a few of them with him! Then three different people told me about the "Redheads." Ralph sees "her" in Box B about 2 AM. Beverly saw "him" in Mezzanine Row H. Cast member Tony Chiroldes has twice felt the presence of his Mom, an actress and also, at times, a redhead. None of these people knew of the others' stories! Our beautiful red theatre must be a beacon for them. I myself, during a company meeting in the house, saw a door open fully and close slowly all by itself, but nervously dismissed it till I heard these stories. However, I was assured that these are benevolent beings that like musicals, as nothing bad ever happens during those times when music fills the Richard Rodgers Theatre.

Also during the run of *In the Heights,* ensemble member Luis Salgado claimed to have seen the ghost of a small child just off stage during a show. Mandy Gonzalez (Nina) said that in the middle of a company meeting in the balcony, an exit door opened on its own with nothing pushing it.

The theatre has more recently been home to *Hamilton*, which has several scenes of ghostly characters speaking from beyond the grave.

Conrad Kemp, the English actor who played Benvolio in the 2013 *Romeo and Juliet* there, explained how he and his countrymen dealt with the ghosts. "We created an Elizabethan bundle (including chocolate, tobacco, splashes of wine, red roses and white, polenta, some choice pieces of text, and some very good will), which we hung in the rafters as a distraction and plaything for all the little mischievous sprites and notions that might otherwise decide to play onstage and cause mishaps. As it turned out, we had quite a few bloody spells despite our bundle. But we all made it out the other end happily and healthily, so perhaps the bundle did keep the naughties mostly occupied."

THE CORT THEATRE

The Cort Theatre, named for West Coast impresario John Cort, used to be part of a cluster of theatres on 48th Street, but on the east side of Times Square. Over the years, the others were knocked down one by one until now, and the Cort stands alone on the border of Rockefeller Center. There is a published story of a female ghost who was raped in the house, and now haunts its backstage area,

During the 2006 revival of *Barefoot in the Park*, production stage manager Valerie A. Peterson reported that props master Steve Loele saw a ghost in the theatre's basement. Not sure if it is the same ghost as the assaulted woman because all he saw was the shape of an invisible person sitting on a sofa facing a television set. When he approached, the soft cushions sprang back up, as if someone was getting up.

It will be interesting to see if audiences and theatre workers notice any Martin Beck- or Henry Miller-style posthumous pique when the Cort is renamed for actor James Earl Jones, as was announced in early 2022.

THE MAJESTIC THEATRE

There's one more kind of ghost I haven't described yet, but which deserves a place alongside the more substantial spirits—if "substantial" is the right word. It is the kind of ghost who lives only in people's memories: friends and coworkers who were so vivid in life, and now passed away.

Kris Koop Ouellette, longtime sweetheart in the ensemble of *The Phantom of the Opera*, wrote that the whole cast of the long-running musical was devastated by the loss of the stage manager, Barbara-Mae Phillips of cancer at age fifty-nine. Ouellette said "the appearance of Barbara-Mae Phillips every time we walk around a corner and used to see her there," is a kind of ghost, too.

SOMETHING CURIOUS

During the decade I was editor of *The Playbill Broadway Yearbook* series, my staff and I did a chapter each year on every show on Broadway. The chapter included not only the cover and contents of every *Playbill* but also photos of everyone who worked on the show—that included not only all the actors but all the creative people, all the stagehands, all the carpenters, lighting folk, concessionaires, and even the stage door-person. I also asked every show to supply a "correspondent"—some-one who worked on the show in any capacity—to survey the cast and answer questions about what life was like backstage, from Who Got the Gypsy Robe, to Special In-Theatre Hangouts to Pre-Show Rituals, and so on. I included one key question: Did they have any ghostly encoun-ters? Many didn't; some did. So, during the ten years I edited the book, I obtained a horizontal and vertical survey of the ghosts at nearly every show at every theatre. Many are quoted in this book.

And I noticed something curious. In year after year, show after show, there were certain theatres that *always* reported ghostly sightings. Moreover, the sightings were pretty consistent. The ghosts materialized at similar times, were similar in appearance and "performed" actions that were similar if not identical in each manifestation. This was true whether my correspondents consulted with one another or not. They came upon these reports more or less independently.

The other interesting thing was that the theatres that *didn't* have ghost stories *never* had ghost stories. The Broadhurst, the Schoenfeld and others. My correspondents in those theatres would say, "Sorry, we've seen nothing."

It's almost as if some theatres actually had ghosts and others didn't—something for the ghost skeptics to reflect upon.

These are beautiful old theatres—from the audience's point of view—and what they hide behind the scenes! As Howard Sherman asked in *Encore Monthly* magazine, "Ever been alone at night in cos-tume or props storage?" Empty costumes, especially when lit by just a work light, somehow retain a little bit of the life left behind by the actors who wore them. These are not ordinary pieces of clothing. Costumes were made to move, made to look their best under colored lights. They don't want to hang still. You can't help but feel them reaching out to you, yearning to be worn on a stage.

The same is true of the props. People fall in love with the theatre. They become enchanted by its magic. Why can't ordinarily inanimate objects become subject to that magic as well? Doors want to be opened. Stoves want to cook something. Stairways want to be climbed.

If you see a teapot, you expect, at some point, tea will be served. But is that teapot really as innocent as it seems? What kind of tea does it contain?

And, of course, guns. They say never to display a gun onstage unless you intend, at some point, to fire it. Guns want to be fired. There is a wonderful trick used in the musical *Assassins*, about presidential assassins and would-be assassins. The trick plays with the audience's feelings about this very quality in a gun. In "Gun Song," the killers sing the praises of the favorite tool of their trade. They sing, "When you've got a gun—" and they suddenly turn and point their weapons at the startled audience. After a taut moment's pause, they continue, "—everybody pays attention." The audience fears, for just a fraction of a second, that there is a real danger that someone onstage might make a mistake, or perhaps go crazy, or perhaps the gun could acquire some kind of evil life of its own, just for that moment. And, after all, this is live theatre. *What's to stop it?*

And then the show continues.

THE TEASPOON BRIGADE

And there may be even more Broadway ghosts coming in the future. During my years at *Playbill* I got wind of a strictly sub-rosa organization called the Teaspoon Brigade. I'm not sure how "organized" this organization is, or if it's just a few ghost-positive theatre folk having what they think is fun.

Each member chooses a theatre—not just any theatre, but their *favorite* theatre. The theatre where they had their happiest memory. The theatre where they wouldn't mind spending eternity because it is the theatre they want someday to *haunt.* They have a collective agreement that when they die their bodies will be cremated and one teaspoon of the ashes will be deposited by their fellow Brigadiers in the theatre they want to haunt. They believe that this will lead to their ghost taking up residence in that theatre.

Anyone who thinks they might like to pursue this interest—and particularly anyone who would want to aid and abet them in carrying out their wishes—should keep in mind that scattering human remains on private property without written permission is a misdemeanor crime in New York, and most states.

For what it's worth, I also am not aware of any time the teaspoon thing ever worked.

So, let's take a look, now, at some other Broadway ghosts that got where they are without the help of criminal silverware.

6

CELEBRITY GHOST STORIES

Just because someone is a famous celebrity doesn't mean they are somehow insulated from backstage encounters with the supernatural.

CAROL CHANNING

Carol Channing parlayed her wild blonde hair, anime-character eyes, shquawking voice, and joyously extroverted manner into a Broadway, TV, and movie career bookended by two landmark performances: Lorelei Lee, who sings "Diamonds Are a Girl's Best Friend" in the 1949 musical *Gentlemen Prefer Blondes*, and Dolly Gallagher Levi, singing "Before the Parade Passes By" in 1964's *Hello, Dolly!*

Like the great vaudeville stars of the past, Channing finally got to play the Palace in New York in 1974 with an updated version of *Gentlemen Prefer Blondes*, retitled *Lorelei*. She said she was well aware of the ghosts at the Palace, especially one, a spirit who seemed to have free run of the theatre. "Usually," she said, "he was wandering around the mezzanine. But at one performance he was in the orchestra pit playing an instrument."

ANDREA MCARDLE

Andrea McArdle originated the role of the curly-haired, red-dressed Little Orphan Annie in the musical *Annie*. Unlike so many other child stars, she made the transition to teenager and then to adult, graduating to Fantine in *Les Misérables*, Ashley the smoking car in *Starlight Express*, Margy in *State Fair*, and other roles. These included, in a regional production, her old nemesis, Miss Hannigan, in *Annie*. One of her stage triumphs was taking over the role of Belle in Disney's *Beauty and the Beast*, which at that time was playing the Palace.

One night, she stayed late in her dressing room and, coming down the stairs after most others had already left, she crossed into the house. There, in the orchestra pit, she saw a startling sight. A man dressed entirely in white was playing furiously on a cello. She stood and listened for a short while. Then, when she saw that he was not stopping anytime soon, she left. As she walked through the wings and toward the stage door, she saw the stage doorman and asked him who's the guy playing cello in the orchestra pit. The doorman didn't bat an eye. He told her she was seeing one of the more unusual ghosts: the Palace's ghost musician.

Was this the same ghost Channing had seen?

CELESTE HOLM

Celeste Holm, the original Ado Annie in *Oklahoma!*, went on to star on Broadway in *Bloomer Girl* and other stage shows, and in *All about Eve*, *Gentlemen's Agreement*, and dozens more movies and TV shows. You would think that someone like that would have seen everything.

But years afterward she still retained a vivid memory of a supernatural encounter she had in 1937, early in her career, at English's Theatre in Indianapolis when she was touring as Crystal in *The Women*.

I was alone on the stage. . . . There was just a work light. Suddenly I was aware of someone sitting in the stage box. He was a man with a goatee; he was wearing steel-rimmed spectacles and a gray suit. I smiled at him but he didn't react.

I went out, through the passdoor [which connects the backstage area and the public part of the theatre] on the side, in order to see the pictures on the walls, of our ancestors, the famous actors who had played at the theatre. Being young, I could see in the dark. I felt a little draft behind my head, the way you do when somebody goes by you. I turned and saw the curtains quiver. He'd left the box.

That Sunday, on the train, somebody asked, "Did anyone see the ghost of Mr. English?" He threw over the program [of the show they were appearing in] to my two roommates and me. We were the youngest members of the company, the "three little pigs." The picture in the program was of the man I'd seen in the box. I started to speak, but before I could get it out, somebody else said, "Oh, he only shows himself to great actors."

I knew I was so far from a great actress, at that point, but I did know how it ought to be. I couldn't do it yet, but I was aimed in the right direction. . . . Whenever I get very discouraged, I do remember that Mr. English allowed me to see him.

LAURA LINNEY

Laura Linney has won awards for her acting in film and TV plus five Tony Award nominations. She collided with one of Broadway's best-known ghosts, the Lady in Blue, when she was appearing at the Belasco Theatre in 1998. "It's absolutely haunted," she told James Corden on *The Late Late Show.* "I was not a believer. I had been told about the ghosts at the Belasco. . . . Legend is that final dress rehearsals, that's when the ghosts come out. I had forgotten this, and I was doing [*Honour*] with Jane Alexander, and I turned to [her], and I looked up to the upper balcony—there are two balconies there—and the upper balcony you can only get in from the outside, and those doors were locked; and I looked up, and there was a woman standing in the front row looking over with a blue dress and blonde hair. I just thought, 'Well, hello!' I looked back at Jane, and I looked back up, and she was gone."

Linney checked to see if her suspicion was accurate. "I went to the house manager and I said, 'Joe, I think I saw a ghost.' And he went, 'male or female?' I said, 'female.' And he went, 'blue dress, blonde hair?'"

The Lady in Blue had struck again.

PATRICK STEWART

Patrick Stewart may be familiar to a mass audience for his memorable performance as Capt. Jean-Luc Picard on the hit TV series *Star Trek: The Next Generation*, but he was trained in the classics and often returns to the stage. He has appeared on Broadway twelve times, in plays by Shakespeare, Pinter, and Mamet. And he saw plenty of Shakespearean ghosts when he starred in *Macbeth* at the haunted Lyceum Theatre in 2008, and in PBS's "Great Performances" production of the same cursed play in 2010.

But Stewart had a real-life ghostly encounter in 2009 when he was costarring with Ian McKellen in Samuel Beckett's *Waiting for Godot* at the Theatre Royal Haymarket in London, which is famously haunted by the spirit of its onetime manager, John Baldwin Buckstone, as I will discuss in a chapter on London theatre ghosts. Stewart recounted the story in a documentary film produced by the Sky Arts television channel.

McKellen noticed that suddenly Stewart seemed distracted in the middle of the show. When intermission rolled around, McKellen asked, "What happened, what threw you?"

"I just saw a ghost. On stage, during Act One," Stewart replied.

Nigel Everett, a director of the theatre, told the *Telegraph* newspaper: "Patrick told us all about it. He was stunned. I would not say frightened, but I would say impressed."

Everett added, "The ghost tends to appear when a comedy is playing." While he said he did not consider *Waiting for Godot* to be a comedy, he thought their production did have comic aspects. "I think Buckstone appears when he appreciates things," he added. "We view it as a positive thing."

Stewart became the latest in a collection of actors including Donald Sinden and Judi Dench, to have run into the talent-appreciating Blackstone.

PATTI LUPONE

In chapter 5 we examined ghostly goings on at the Eugene O'Neill Theatre. Donna Lynne Champlin, who played Pirelli in the innovative

2006 production of *Sweeney Todd*, told this story, involving the show's costar Patti LuPone, who played Mrs. Lovett in the cannibalism-themed musical: "Patti's dressing room has doors that open and close on their own. She also thought she had stepped backward onto her friend's foot, so she said, 'Excuse me.' Her friend said, 'What for?' Patti turned around and her friend was a good two feet away from her."

MELISSA ERRICO

The 2004 production *Dracula, The Musical* also seems to have inspired David Belasco, whom we met in chapter 3. Leading lady Melissa Errico, who starred on Broadway as Eliza Doolittle in the 1993 revival of *My Fair Lady*, and has gone on to topline *High Society*, *Amour* (Tony Award Nomination for Best Leading Actress), and *Irving Berlin's White Christmas*, got a chance to meet the Bishop of Broadway personally.

Playing Mina in the 2004 Frank Wildhorn *Dracula* musical, Errico said she heard the muffled sounds of a loud argument coming from behind a large painting of Belasco that hangs just inside the stage door. When she asked the doorman whose dressing room was behind the painting, she was told that there was no room at all behind there. The source of the argument was never discovered.

Errico told *Playbill* that Belasco does indeed haunt the theatre. "My dresser Cathy saw him walk into a mirror the other day. She thinks he lives in the mirror in the wall outside my dressing room. One night I forgot my coat and I had turned out the lights in my room. I turned back to get my coat in the dark and someone (David?) turned the small pretty table light on for me to see my way. It was spooky! As I opened the door to leave, as I was walking out, 'someone' closed the door behind me. I didn't touch it but watched it move."

Getting into the spirit of their supernatural musical, the cast of *Dracula* celebrated Belasco's 150th birthday with a cake and sang "Happy Birthday" to him.

BRIAN STOKES MITCHELL

Brian Stokes Mitchell was the star of Broadway's *Ragtime, Kiss of the Spider-Woman*, and many other plays and musicals, including a revival of *Kiss Me, Kate* that won him the Tony Award as Best Leading Actor in a Musical. Known as "Stokes" to theatre folk, he has worked in many theatres over his long career, which prompted him to notice something interesting. In the preface to *At This Theatre*, a book that traces the history of each of the Broadway theatres, Mitchell wrote,

> The concept of spirits and theatre intermingled is part of the history, tradition and superstition of the theatre that follows us into this 21st century. Every night, after the audience has left and the stage lights and house lights are extinguished, the house electrician places a single light on stage. It is usually a large black lamp about five feet tall with a single bare light bulb on top. It is there to illuminate the way for the actors who are yet removing makeup and costumes and crew members that are performing their final duties of the evening. It remains on throughout the night and the next day and is not turned off until the stage lights are once again brought to life in preparation for the next show.

It is called the ghost light.

There is debate on exactly how it got its name. Some say it is because of its ghostly glow and the long shadows it casts. Others say it is there to keep away certain mischievous spirits that may lurk in the aisles or dressing rooms or backstage nooks. Still others say it is there as a beacon to the ghosts of the theatre who wish never to be left in darkness. I like to think it is a beacon.

I am generally one of the last people out of the theatre. I love crossing the dimly lit stage while making my way to the final exit of the evening out the stage door. Oftentimes I stop at the center of the stage while bathed in the soft glow of the ghost light and I stand silently for a few minutes, staring out into an empty house that fades into darkness. That's when I can best feel the spirit of the theatre and the ghosts that reside there. In those quiet moments, one can't help but hear the echoes of voices long gone—the words and music and laughter and applause that once resounded within those same walls.

I can nearly hear the excited backstage whispers of "Merde!" and "Break a leg!" I can almost feel the footfalls of other performers who once walked those same boards. I can smell the paint and sawdust and the burnt gels of the lights; the pipe and cigar smoke that once emanated from the lobby. I catch a fleeting glimpse of something beautiful trying to escape notice in the wings. These are the ghosts that become illuminated for me.

And Mitchell added a little free-verse poem about the future:

Perhaps one day my spirit will join my fellows
Released from the wood and metal and plaster and stone,
Summoned by the ghost light
And the optimistic hearts that beckon us
As we welcome in support a new Act
In the continuing story of body and mind and heart and soul
That once again plays
"At this theatre."

7

OFF-BROADWAY GHOSTS

Off-Broadway has its share of ghosts, too. Broadway and off-Broadway are distinguished primarily by contract, by seating capacity, and, to a lesser but more public degree, by location.

There are only three Broadway theatres actually located on Broadway: the Winter Garden, the Minskoff, and the aptly named Broadway. Most Broadway theatres are located on the blocks surrounding Times Square, but not all. One is a mile north at Lincoln Center, the Beaumont.

Off-Broadway theatres on the other hand are clustered here and there around Manhattan Island. One cluster ("Theatre Row") is found on far West 42nd Street. A few theatres remain of the classic old Greenwich Village cluster, though many have been lost. Another cluster happens to be located, perversely, around Times Square.

Many off-Broadway houses were not originally built as theatres. They are repurposed churches or warehouses or other quirky spaces, like an underground former cinema complex and even an old beauty school. Some of them are a century or more old. These spaces bring along their own histories and secrets and, often, ghosts.

THE CHERRY LANE THEATRE

On a crooked little street in the heart of Greenwich Village stands the legendary Cherry Lane Theatre, like a very dignified and classy old lady who was a beatnik in her youth. The theatre was founded in 1924 by poet Edna St. Vincent Millay, who lived around the corner (and is said to haunt that building as well).

Many future writing and designing stars got their start or stretched their muscles there: Eugene O'Neill, Amiri Baraka, Edward Albee, Gertrude Stein, Elmer Rice, Clifford Odets, William Saroyan, Lorraine Hansberry, Samuel Beckett, David Mamet, Sam Shepard, and a full house more. Think of the vibrations that group has been bringing the Cherry Lane.

Over the century since the theatre opened, people have seen eddies of white mist moving across the stage or the top of the lobby staircase, and a shadow that appears near the dressing room—with nothing seeming to cast the shadow. Perhaps some of them encountered the mirror ghost: while actors are getting made up, they see faces staring back at them and then melting away.

Author L'Aura Hladik interviewed Alex, the Cherry Lane's manager, who said he's seen nothing paranormal at the theatre . . . but isn't taking any chances. "We like to think that the spirit of Edna [Millay] keeps an eye on the place. I always say, 'Good morning, Edna,' or 'Good night, Edna.' when coming or going."

Another fun ghost connection: in 2015 the Cherry Lane booked *Ghostlight 9: A Musical Ghost Story* by Michael Wolk—a musical biography of the New Amsterdam's Olive Thomas.

THE PUBLIC THEATER

The Public Theater is a warren of small off-Broadway and off-off-Broadway theatres just south of Astor Place in the Village.

The Public is technically a not-for-profit theatre, staging daring, experimental, and offbeat shows, especially by women and minority playwrights. But along the way it has managed to incubate shows that moved uptown and became some of the biggest hits on Broadway in the late twentieth and early twenty-first centuries. *Hair, A Chorus Line*, and *Hamilton* are just the biggest three of their "experiments" that became wild commercial successes and changed American theatre.

Built in 1853 as the Astor Library, the future Public Theater was not a public library as we know them today. It was a private reference library endowed by John Jacob Astor for the use of wealthy patrons, Ivy League scholars, and his personal friends, though it was technically open to the public. Books could be consulted on the premises, but not taken out. After Astor and his heirs were gone, the building passed through several hands, including the New York Public Library system, which moved all the books out of the expensive-to-maintain building. In 1920 it was taken over by the Hebrew Immigrant Aid Society, which benefited poor newcomers to the United States—exactly the sort Astor would not have welcomed to his library. The spirits of some of these ragged people still cling to the building, especially its upper floors where some were housed when they had no place else to go.

Another nineteenth century refugee, merchant Austin L. Sands, is believed to stalk the hallways of the Public Theatre, frightening actors and maintenance workers.

The building was facing demolition when energetic and determined producer Joseph Papp discovered it and persuaded New York City to landmark the building and lease it to him and his New York Shakespeare Festival. The NYSF had become known for staging free Shakespeare in Central Park in the mid-1950s, a tradition that continues in the 2020s. Papp saw it as a place where he could tap into the daring and free-spirited theatre community blossoming in the Village in the 1960s. But for all the renovations the building has gone through since Papp began turning its reading rooms into playhouses, it doesn't seem to have shaken a few stubborn ghosts from its Astor Library days. And it may have added a new one—Papp himself.

Papp died in 1991 and passed directorship of the theatre to other hands. But, according to author Dr. Philip Schoenberg, "In recent years, staff members have sometimes caught sight of a familiar if unsubstantive figure as they make their rounds. Theatregoers, too, occasionally spot the man, almost always dressed in a signature white suit, his piercing eyes surveying the room. By the time any of them recognizes the phantom as Papp from the old posters and photographs on display, the guardian spirit has gone."

THE NEW VICTORY THEATER

Among contemporary off-Broadway dramatists who have fashioned interesting new ghost stories, we must turn first to Mac Wellman, whose *Crowbar* explored the idea seriously, and in a uniquely appropriate environment.

The play told the story of hauntings and ghostly presences at the Victory Theater, one of the old legitimate theatres that once formed a

Side-by-side 42nd Street entrances to the Lyric Theatre and the New Victory Theater. Photo by Robert Viagas

sort of Broadway Pantheon of great marble-faced buildings along West 42nd Street, for many years fallen into disrepair and occupied by XXX-rated and/or violent films. Located at 209 West 42nd Street in Manhattan, the Victory was now heading for a rare happy ending. It was being renovated and reborn as part of a larger plan to rescue all of the run-down 200 block of 42nd Street, known as "The Deuce."

Crowbar introduces us to the ghosts who might be haunting such a theatre, a kaleidoscopic nonlinear revue about the lives of the managers, performers, musicians, and others who once stalked the aisles and backstage hallways . . . and perhaps still do. Some were familiar. Oscar Hammerstein (the manager, Oscar I, not his grandson, the lyricist Oscar II) had built the theatre. David Belasco, namesake of the theatre two blocks away, once operated it. Both men's ghosts were included in *Crowbar*.

To top it off, En Garde Arts, the off-Broadway company sponsoring the production, came up with a glitteringly meta idea: they arranged with the owners of the Victory to tell the story of *Crowbar* on its very stage.

One of the many great images and speeches to come out of the play is this from the character "Mr. Rioso" (say it out loud) who speaks of all theatre ghosts as he pinpoints the source of the ghosts of New York. He stops by a strange door—an "ominous door" in the script—inside the 23rd Street subway station.

> This strange door, this strange door bearing the cryptic legend "Night Forces Structure," marks the entrance to the ghost world. From there, they scratch their way, through unknown tunnels and passages, here, to the basement of this place exhausted. Why? The souls of the dead are hungry for stories of the dead, and fires, disasters, catastrophes of every kind.

In the meantime, a happy (perhaps a bit too happy) fate lay around the corner for the Victory. It was rescued, renovated, redeemed, and turned to a use that few would have anticipated during its Burlesque years—a theatre specially tuned to children, now rechristened the New Victory Theater.

PEPPER'S GHOST

Let's conclude this chapter with a ghost that is not a ghost.

Ghosts have been appearing and disappearing on stage with startling regularity since the mid-nineteenth century. How does this happen? High tech, no doubt? Holograms perhaps? No, just a basic, old-fashioned, fool-the-eye theatre trick known to the profession as Pepper's Ghost.

The effect is named for British showman and scientist John Henry Pepper (1821–1900) who developed and popularized it in the 1860s, though the same type of illusion was first documented in 1584 by Neapolitan innovator Giambattista della Porta, whose many contributions to stagecraft were listed in his book *Magia Naturalis* (*Natural Magic*). Pepper did so well with it in his ghost-crazed stage era (see "Phantasmagoria" in chapter 9), that he eventually patented the process, along with coinventor Henry Dircks, who had developed something similar at about the same time.

Quite simply, an actor hiding in a dark space offstage or below the stage is illuminated with a bright light. The lighted actor is reflected through the wings or through a concealed opening in the stage onto a transparent (and therefore effectively invisible) pane of glass interposed between the actor and the audience. The brightly lit figure then appears on the glass and can be made to materialize and dematerialize by gradually brightening or dimming the light.

You may have seen something similar yourself if you've ever noticed a brightly lit object behind you reflected in a glass window in front of you. The effect is still widely used in live concerts and amusement parks, and is precisely the technique used in politicians' teleprompters so they can read the text of their speeches without having to hold a sheaf of papers or constantly look up and down.

Even the Harry Potter franchise has employed this classic illusion. "The Wizarding World of Harry Potter" attraction at the Universal Orlando Resort in Orlando, Florida, uses it on people standing in line for the "Ride the Hogwarts Express" experience. To people at the back of the line, it looks like the people at the front of line are passing through a solid brick wall to access "Track 9¾," as the characters do in the Potter movies. This mirage is created by Pepper's Ghost.

When done well, Pepper's Ghost can still elicit gasps even among jaded modern audiences. A recent Broadway musical that dealt extensively with the supernatural ended with a couple, consisting of a live woman and the ghost of her sweetheart, embracing and kissing goodbye. Then, seemingly with no set pieces nearby, the man waved farewell and vanished from the center of the stage to the verbal astonishment of the audience. I don't mention the title of the play because the special effects people never confirmed that this was a Pepper's Ghost effect. But that is exactly the kind of thing Pepper's Ghost does best.

8

HAUNTED U.S. THEATRES OF THE EAST

Dozens of theatres across the United States claim to be haunted. This chapter will tell some of the more beguiling stories from states east of the Mississippi River.

THE FOX THEATRE, ATLANTA

The "Fabulous Fox" Theatre in Atlanta is said to be haunted by several ghosts according to Jamie Vosmeier, vice president of sales and marketing, who maintains a list of sightings at the ninety-year-old playhouse. He said the ghost of a little girl, believed to be the daughter of the family that owned and farmed the land where the Fox now stands, appears to backstage workers, accompanied by the distinctive sound of a bouncing ball. She is sometimes glimpsed skipping through the theatre's basement.

Roosevelt, the first African American ghost on this list, haunts the sub-basement boiler room where he shoveled coal in the 1930s and 1940s. Doors are seen to open and close by themselves where there is no draft to push them. Vosmeier said, "Once, when one of the guys who worked down there called out, 'Roosevelt, prove you're here,' a screwdriver rolled off a bench by itself. Everyone left the room."

The Fox holds two other distinctions: It has a haunted infirmary, leftover from the days when wealthy patrons were sometimes overcome with heat, overeating, or drink. The Fox also boasts a haunted Möller pipe organ. Known as "Mighty Mo," the majestic instrument is said to be haunted by the ghost of one of its longtime organists.

THE IROQUOIS THEATRE, CHICAGO

Most ghosts are solitary. There are a few here and there who share their haunted spaces with one or more other wandering spirits. But most of them died alone and spend their twilight afterlife in solitary, accompanied only by the living, from whom they are forever separated.

One of the most horrifying exceptions is at the old Iroquois Theatre, which stood at 24-48 West Randolph Street in Chicago. Six hundred and two theatregoers perished together in the December 1903 fire at the newly built theatre—more than the amount of people who died in the Great Chicago Fire of 1871.

Blame it, perhaps, on the same early-twentieth-century hubris that led the builders of the *Titanic* to boast that the doomed luxury liner was "unsinkable." The theatre was advertised as "absolutely fireproof"—a potent drawing card in a time before government-mandated sprinkler systems, alarms, hose systems, or emergency lighting. The old theatres were firetraps in many ways. Aside from being made largely of wood, the buildings were filled with canvas flats, hemp ropes, and costumes made of flammable material. On top of that, theatres had for years been lit by candles, superseded by gas flame, superseded by primitive electricity. The stage itself was lit by "limelight," a system of burning ingots of lime focused on the stage by mirrors. No wonder so few pre-1900 theatre buildings still exist.

By the turn of the twentieth century, theatre designers were making efforts to counteract these problems, and the Iroquois claimed to have the latest, including a supposedly fireproof asbestos curtain, designed to separate the stage from the audience and compartmentalize any potential fire.

But on December 30, 1903, just thirty-seven days after the theatre opened its doors for the first time, a holiday-season matinee crowd packed the theatre to see the children's show *Mr. Blue Beard*, starring the popular comedian Eddie Foy. The theatre had an orchestra section on the main floor with two balconies above, and all were cleanly sold out, with many more spectators crowded in the back in standing room. It is estimated that there were more than two thousand souls in the building. So many extra tickets had been sold for that performance that people were allowed to sit in the aisles, further blocking egress. Under pressure to finish quickly, architect Benjamin Marshall had ignored Chicago city fire regulations that required separate exits for each level.

During the second act, one of the arc lights sparked and set a cloth drop on fire above the stage. The much-touted asbestos curtain got snagged and could not be closed. Afterward, inspectors could find no trace of the curtain, which apparently burned along with everything else, and concluded it hadn't been made of asbestos after all, or had been made of asbestos mixed with flammable materials.

As the flames mounted and spread both into the house and onto the canvas stage sets, smoke began to fill the playhouse. Panicked audience members raced to escape, creating a bottleneck at the theatre's only regular exit. The few other fire exits were found to be locked, likely to prevent people sneaking into the performance. Windows within reach of the orchestra section were closed from the outside with heavily bolted sheet iron doors.

Foy himself is still regarded as a hero of the disaster. He remained on the stage, trying to calm and direct the increasingly hysterical crowds even as the stage began to burn around him. Foy's actions during the fire were dramatized in the 1955 Bob Hope film *The Seven Little Foys*, named after his family vaudeville act. Foy and his son were among those able to escape the Iroquois conflagration, but many others were not so lucky.

There was little more he could have done. People in the balconies tried to clamber down the staircases to escape, only to find locked iron gates blocking their way, installed by the management to keep people in the cheap seats from sneaking downstairs after the lights went down.

They then tried to exit onto the fire escapes, only to find that they had not been completed and the ladders could not be lowered. As the inferno intensified, people caught between the heat of the fire and ice-coated fire escapes began to jump, landing hard on the alleyway beside the theatre. More than a hundred people leaped to their deaths.

Some tried to escape through the stage door, which only opened inward. The press of people made pulling the door inward impossible.

There was no direct telephone connection from the theatre to the Chicago Fire Department. By the time firefighters arrived, they were witnesses to a catastrophe.

In the end, the areas inside the doors were reported to have been piled seven feet deep in dead bodies, many killed by smoke inhalation or simply crushed by the press of the crowd. Too many of them were youngsters brought there by their parents for a fun afternoon. For many years, the Iroquois fire was listed as the deadliest building fire in U.S. history. It's still in the top ten.

The shell of the Iroquois was demolished. A new theatre was built on the site, christened the Oriental Theatre, and today is known as the James M. Nederlander Theatre. It is booked with major national tours by Broadway Across America. But the dead aren't fooled. While many theatregoers today see great contemporary productions there without incident, workers say they still sometimes hear the muttering of voices, soft footfalls, and distant applause of a crowd, even when the theatre is empty. Furthermore, a sobbing woman in white is sometimes seen wandering the alleyway where so many plunged to their deaths. It acquired the sobriquet "Death Alley."

The Iroquois's many ghosts are known to wander the backstage area as well. *Conde Nast Traveler* reported that actress Ana Gasteyer, a graduate of *Saturday Night Live*, claims to have "gotten the creeps" while appearing there in a sit-down production of *Wicked* in the late 2000s. Gasteyer described her experience on an episode of Bio channel's "Celebrity Ghost Stories" series, as reported by Deena Budd on BellaOnline:

> Ana [Gasteyer] first mentioned the now rarely used back alley called "Death Alley" since the Iroquois Theater fire when the bodies were stacked there by the firemen. She described the alley as being "very dismal and gloomy." She said that it felt terrible to be there.
>
> On December 30th, the anniversary of the fire, Ana had a paranormal experience during her performance at the theatre.

At the end of Act I, her character, the witch Elphaba is learning to fly, and she flies up high into the air. There is a great deal of fog and smoke, and the orchestra is playing very loudly.

While flying up into the air, Ana noticed a lot of people in the wings standing in little groups. After the show, she is walking down a long deserted hallway to her dressing room, when she hears children crying. A moment later, she sees a woman and two children standing at the end of the hallway dressed in winter period clothing. The family appears calm and collected, but out of place. The mother, especially, exudes sadness. Ana nods to the woman, who nods back. They then turn a corner, and disappear. Ana has no doubt that this family perished in the fire of 1903. She said that *Wicked* is a play for families and children, and it stands to reason that the ghosts of other mothers and children would be joining them nightly.

So let's put the restless Iroquois Theatre spirits in the category of souls who passed over abruptly before their natural time. If there is any silver lining at all, the disaster led to tougher fire regulations in Chicago and across the United States. And at least the theatre-loving ghost audience gets to watch every show that comes through, for free, forever.

VICTORY GARDENS BIOGRAPH THEATER, CHICAGO, ILLINOIS

One of the most charismatic Chicago theatre ghosts is Depression-era celebrity bank robber John Dillinger—or is it?

Back in 1934, the scandal sheets of the time breathlessly reported his daring daylight felonies and audacious escapes from the law across Illinois, Indiana, and Ohio. Dillinger's notoriety and antihero fan base was increased by the fact that he sometimes shared his "earnings" with the Depression-beset poor of Chicago—making him a kind of modern-day Robin Hood.

His crime stats began to pile up. Following two arrests and two escapes from prison (he boasted that no jail could hold him), he and his gang robbed a dozen banks, along the way killing two cops, two FBI agents, and an innocent member of the public in the wrong place at the wrong time. To help hide his identity, Dillinger reportedly underwent plastic surgery—which included altering his fingerprints.

Undeterred, the FBI made it a priority to put an end to his spree, naming Dillinger "Public Enemy Number One."

On the warm evening of July 22, Dillinger decided to spend some of his ill-gotten gains on a night out at the movies, with not one but two female companions. The 1914-vintage Biograph Theater (today known as the Victory Gardens Biograph Theater) was showing *Manhattan Melodrama* that night.

Someone—many people believe it was one of those companions—tipped the G-men, who were waiting when Dillinger and dates emerged into the alleyway beside the Biograph. He responded to the command to surrender by pulling a hidden gun and trying another of his Houdini-like escapes. The cops didn't like that, and Dillinger died from a single lump of constabulary lead at age thirty-one.

According to Ashley Powers of Architecture.org, "he fell at the feet of a theatre patron, a woman who had known him as a young man.

She was interviewed by a newspaper, where she repeated his last words, 'They finally got me.'"

Maybe they did—and maybe they didn't. Apparently Dillinger never stopped running. Ever since that night at the movies, people visiting the Biograph have witnessed a figure variously described as "shadowy" and "bluish" dashing through the alley and falling before disappearing. Paranormal activity inside the theatre and in the alleyway reportedly increased after renovations in the 1970s and in 2006, including unexplained icy-cold spots. Perhaps no jail could hold him, but he appears to be trapped for eternity in that forlorn alley.

Here's the interesting twist. Many of Dillinger's followers still believe that it wasn't the famous robber at all who took the bullet. It was a patsy named Jimmy Lawrence who was set up to die in his place, so Dillinger could give up his life of crime and live peacefully far from the spotlight, as many Elvis Presley fans believe of their idol today. The plastic surgery helped support the rumor that it was the wrong corpse at the morgue.

So, in this case, the existence of a ghost isn't the question—since so many have seen it—but is it Dillinger or someone else?

THE NATIONAL THEATRE, WASHINGTON, DC

As we've seen, not all theatre ghosts take tragic or villainous roles.

Stage folk at the National Theatre in Washington, DC, are generally happy about their ghost—though he can sometimes startle them—because he once was one of them. It seems that he's *still* one of them.

Roll back to the late 1800s when an actor named John McCullough was doing his wash in a creek that ran under the theatre where he was performing. A fellow actor, but a rival in romance, argued with

McCullough over the woman, plugged him, and, in a melodramatic flourish not unknown in his profession, buried his victim in the dirt floor under what was then the stage.

Sad and ghastly, of course. The killer was caught and punished. But what theatre ghost was ever so perfectly prepared for his posthumous role?

In a lively and detailed story in the *Washington Post*, writer Pamela Whitehead tracked down the facts about McCullough. She reports that the ghost appears to be costumed as Hamlet. He's reported to be "very peaceful," not a scary ghost at all. He was well known to the people he encountered, and that live-and-let-be-dead attitude has been handed down to the janitors, watchmen and stage doormen who report seeing "the outline of a man" inside the National in recent years. He makes his most frequent appearances on or near opening nights.

What's surprising about his appearance is that several theatre buildings have fallen and risen on that site since his death and before the National was built there. McCullough may be an industry-specific ghost, but apparently not a building-specific one. In 1978 he was seen crossing the stage in costume and vanishing, as witnessed by fellow actor Frederic Bond.

Hearing the stories and accounts of the sightings, former manager Edmund Plohn resolved to see if there really was a body buried in his basement and, if so, to reinter him someplace more traditional, not to say legal. A more recent manager, Scott Kirkpatrick, said he was instantly tangled in red tape over an unaccounted corpse that he wasn't even sure was there.

In the end, it all came down to the actors. People who worked at the theatre protested McCullough's potential removal. So no action was taken. The plot of earthen floor in the basement kept its secret. Whether the body is there or not, a part of McCullough seems very much at home there.

FORD'S THEATRE, WASHINGTON, DC

Speaking of actors, we now come to another Washington, DC, theatre. It is said to be haunted by one or perhaps two of the most famous ghosts in American history.

Abraham Lincoln was a devoted theatregoer, from his days in Springfield, Illinois, though he didn't have much of an assortment beyond amateur productions and minstrel shows, whose corny style of humor influenced his own throughout his life.

After he was elected president in 1860, he began to appreciate higher-toned fare, eventually coming to enjoy Shakespeare, whose work added to his store of aphorisms. He attended the theatre and the opera, often with Mary Lincoln or political friends.

Shakespeare's words—and the thoughts and feelings behind the words—impressed themselves on the president profoundly. Shortly after the death of his son Willie, Lincoln and his companions were on a military cruise to a captured Virginia seaport. To pass the time, Lincoln read aloud to his guests from *Hamlet*, *Macbeth*, and *King Lear*, but, according to Thomas A. Bogar's *American Presidents Attend the Theatre*, "His companions were most moved by his reciting from memory a passage from *King John* in which Constance laments the death of her son: 'I have heard you say that we shall see and know our friends in heaven. If that is true, I shall see my boy again.' Turning to an aide, he mused, 'Did you ever dream of a lost friend and feel that you were holding

Portrait of Olive Thomas that hangs inside the stage door of the New Amsterdam Theatre so company members can greet her with a "Good morning, Olive" when they arrive for work. Photo by Robert Viagas

The portrait of Olive Thomas that hangs in the lobby of Disney's New Amsterdam Theatre. Photo by Robert Viagas

Olive Thomas (circa 1920s). Photofest

Olive Thomas, early in life (circa 1920s). Photofest

David Belasco, circa
1910s. Photofest

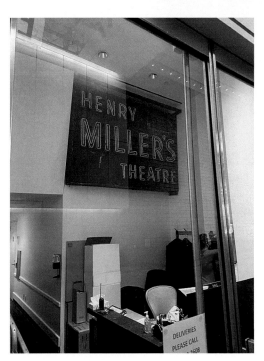

The stage door
entrance to the Stephen
Sondheim Theatre, with
the sign from when
the theatre was called
Henry Miller's Theatre.
Photo by Robert Viagas

Keyboardist Ken Double and the "Mighty Mo," the haunted pipe organ at the Fox Theatre in Atlanta. Photo by Tim Stephens

Author Robert Viagas with the ghost light of the Cherry Lane Theatre in Greenwich Village. Photo by Robert Viagas

Melissa Errico and Tom Hewitt in *Dracula, The Musical* (2004) at the Belasco Theatre. Photo by Joan Marcus

The marquee of Broadway's Al Hirschfeld Theatre, showing the neon sign with artist Hirschfeld dipping a pen into his head. Photo by Robert Viagas

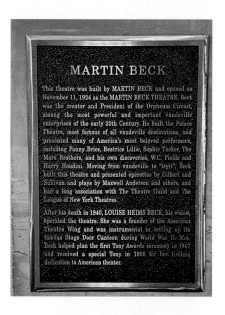

Plaque that greets playgoers to the renamed Al Hirschfeld Theatre on Broadway, telling the story of the original owner and namesake, Martin Beck. Photo by Robert Viagas

An illustration showing an artist's impression of the Iroquois Theatre fire in Chicago, 1904. Chronicle/Alamy Stock Photo

A painting depicting assassin John Wilkes Booth leaping from the house-right box after he fatally shot President Abraham Lincoln at Ford's Theatre on April 14, 1865, in Washington, DC. Heritage Image Partnership Ltd/Alamy Stock Photo

The legendary Palace Theatre in Times Square, shrouded in scaffolding as the whole building is being jacked up in 2022 to make room for retail space on the ground level. Photo by Robert Viagas

Cover of the book *Mosby, the Kennedy Center Cat*. Photo by Robert Viagas

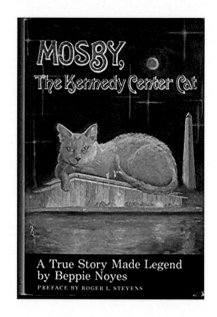

Harry Houdini in chains, circa 1899. Photofest

Display case containing Olive Thomas memorabilia at the New Amsterdam Theatre in New York. Used by permission from Disney Theatricals. Photo by Robert Viagas

sweet communion with that friend, and yet have a sad consciousness that it was not a reality? Just so I dream of my boy Willie.' Observers report that as he said these words 'his great frame shook and bowing down on the table he wept as only such a man in the [breaking] down of great sorrow could weep.'"

On Monday April 9, 1865, the day Confederate General Robert E. Lee surrendered to General Ulysses S. Grant, Lincoln again turned to the Bard. His choices included Macbeth's speech following his assassination of King Duncan as he slept, in which he compares death and sleep. "Sleep that soothes away all our worries. Sleep that puts each day to rest. . . . Sleep, the main course in life's feast, and the most nourishing."

A witness said Lincoln praised "Shakespeare's skill in providing a precise picture 'of a murderer's mind when the dark deed achieved, its perpetrator already envies his victim's calm sleep.' He read the scene over twice."

Perhaps the president was thinking of a dream he had had the previous week. Lincoln's friend Ward Hill Lamon said that Lincoln had dreamed his own death. "According to Lamon, the president had a dream in which he heard many [people] mourning, whining and crying. On a catafalque in the East Room of the White House, a coffin. Lincoln asked a soldier, who was standing guard over the body, who the corpse was. The Soldier would then have replied: the president. He was murdered."

That woke Lincoln, who was disturbed enough by it that he shared it with Lamon on April 11. Perhaps it was not a premonition of any kind. Death threats against him were incessant. As president, Lincoln had watched hundreds of thousands of Americans die under his command. He had lost his son. Funerals were everywhere.

Lincoln knew a sure way to relax though. Go out and see a show.

Among the many shows he had attended during his presidency was *The Marble Heart*, featuring one of the hot actors of the day, John Wilkes Booth, of the theatrical Booth family. Broadway still has a Booth Theatre, which is named for his brother, Edwin (more on a ghost at that theatre in chapter 5).

John Wilkes knew the president was going to be in the house. According to a famous story from Lincoln's sister-in-law, Emilie Todd Helm, "Booth seemed particularly antagonistic towards Lincoln as he performed. So heated were his glares that when his lines included threats, Mrs. Helm told the president, 'Mr. Lincoln, he looks as if he meant that for you.' Lincoln replied, 'He does look pretty sharp at me, doesn't he?'"

Booth was a nineteenth-century QAnon type who was fiercely devoted to the lost Confederate cause, a white supremacist who therefore fiercely hated Lincoln. He tracked Lincoln's movements in the weeks before the Southern surrender and afterward, and got word that the Lincolns and their guests, Major Henry Rathbone and his fiancée, Clara Harris, had decided to go to the theatre Friday, April 14.

The Lincolns had originally planned to see *Aladdin!; or, The Wonderful Lamp*, just as they might have seen the same story recently on Broadway, but Mrs. Lincoln decided she would rather go to another show, as a favor to Laura Keene, manager of the company, for whom the performance was a benefit. Her company was ensconced at Ford's Theatre, performing a surefire popular 1852 comedy *Our American Cousin*, about a snooty English family who get their comeuppance from the crude but crafty American relative they didn't know they had. The show had played Washington before, and Keene was hoping for a big crowd. The Lincolns often attended such benefits, announcing them widely, because they knew their attendance would draw a bigger crowd. It was their kind favor to the theatre world.

That's how Booth found out about it. He made a plan. He knew every inch of Ford's Theatre, because he played there frequently, and sometimes hung out there with friends on the crew. Booth had a horse waiting for him at the stable in the back of the theatre. He entered the building and slipped backstage. No one stopped him because most people knew him, and he knew the most direct route to the back of the stage-left Box Seven (actually Boxes Seven and Eight combined, to accommodate the foursome), where the presidential party sat.

Lincoln reportedly had sent his only guard, DC police officer John Parker, to take a seat in the orchestra and enjoy the show. Parker is believed to have taken the opportunity to leave the building altogether, and went to a tavern next door for a drink.

But Booth stayed. He waited until act III and slipped into the back of the unguarded box. Booth, who knew the play well, waited for the line, "Don't know the manners of good society, eh? Well, I guess I know enough to turn you inside-out, old gal—you sockdologizing old man trap!," which he knew always got a big laugh.

As the wave of laughter rolled through Ford's Theatre, Booth pointed a pistol at the back of Lincoln's head and fired. Lincoln died laughing.

Ever the melodramatist, Booth then leaped to the stage, breaking a bone in his leg in the process, and uttered a line inspired by Shakespeare. The line, "Sic semper tyrannis!" ("Ever thus to tyrants!"), was said to have been uttered by Marcus Brutus after he led a conspiracy to assassinate Rome's Julius Caesar. Booth had played Mark Antony in a production of Shakespeare's *Julius Caesar*, and was aware of the connection. Booth died while on the run from the crime, shot while hiding in a Virginia barn surrounded by unsympathetic soldiers—which brings us to the ghosts.

Lincoln drew his last breath in the bedroom of a private house across from Ford's Theatre, where he was carried after the attack. Lincoln's ghost has been seen and felt there—but in several other places as well.

He's especially active at the White House itself, where he's been seen by President Theodore Roosevelt and First Ladies Grace Coolidge and Lady Bird Johnson. His stovepipe-hatted figure famously appeared to Queen Wilhelmina of the Netherlands when she was visiting the executive mansion, and, memorably, to Winston Churchill, the British prime minister, who had just emerged from a bath and was standing naked when Lincoln appeared in the room with him. The unflappable Churchill reportedly said, "Good evening, Mr. President. You seem to have me at a disadvantage." Lincoln, who apparently still enjoyed a good joke, smiled and dematerialized.

Even when his visage is not seen, he manifests by knocking on doors, footsteps up and down the empty White House stairs, and sometimes by a "presence" felt by those who live and work in the building, including Eleanor Roosevelt and Maureen Reagan.

One can only imagine what Lincoln must think of some recent tenants there.

At Ford's Theatre itself, footsteps are often heard running up the stairs to the area behind the presidential box, which is now hung with bunting and off-limits to the public. The footsteps are commonly believed to be those of assassin Booth. These are sometimes followed by the sound of a distant gunshot and screams. A figure resembling Booth has been seen fleeing across the stage and disappearing into the wings.

The specter of Mary Todd Lincoln has been seen in Box Seven pointing toward the empty stage, and has been heard to shout, "He has killed the president," condemned to relive the greatest moment of horror and sorrow in her supremely difficult life.

Historian Virginia Lamkin, who has written extensively about ghosts, had this account: "Before Ford's Theatre closed in 2007 for major renovations, I took groups of around 100 teenage students over several Spring Breaks to tour Washington, DC. Ford's Theatre was always one of our stops. We always ended up in the basement in the long lines waiting for the single-stall restrooms. Every time I was in this area, I really got some intense, creepy feelings. I have always wondered if some of the items in the basement museum are haunted. Each time I have been in this area since 2009, to attend plays, et cetera. I get the same overwhelming feelings. So when I was doing research . . . I was surprised to find no one else has experienced these same feelings or mentioned this area of the theatre as being haunted."

Postscript: Ford's Theatre itself, which had been one of the most successful theatres in the nation's capital at the time of the assassination, ceased showing plays for many years. Ford's was taken over by the government and used for offices and storage. In 1893, part of the building collapsed, killing twenty-two war department clerks and adding to the building's grisly toll. In 1932 a museum devoted to Lincoln was opened on the main floor, and in 1933 the National Park Service began a renovation to turn the building back into a theatre. The project wasn't completed until 1968.

Ford's Theatre now operates as a full-time legitimate playhouse. Many people work on, and attend, full-scale productions of contemporary dramas and comedies there and experience no supernatural visitations and nothing creepy—other than the somber American flag bunting and a presidential portrait—of George Washington, not Lincoln—on Box Seven-Eight. The portrait is the same one that was there in Lincoln's time, and a visible nick on the frame is said by theatre legend to have been inflicted by Booth's spur as he leaped from the box to the stage.

BOSTON UNIVERSITY THEATRE, BOSTON, MASSACHUSETTS

The playhouse now known as Boston University Theatre (home of the resident troupe, the Huntington Theatre Company) was built in 1923 at the behest of Henry Jewett, a charismatic Australian-born impresario who founded his own company, the Henry Jewett Players, in Boston in 1915. The Players had been performing at the Boston Opera House and various other locales until they earned enough esteem (and money) to build their own permanent home. The company focused on then-new dramas by Ibsen, Shaw, Wilde, and Barrie, usually performed on alternating weeks, and did well during the 1920s. But the Great Depression (and the rise of the movie business) choked off its audience and by 1930 the company was forced to declare bankruptcy.

Jewett had poured his heart and soul into the Players, and the company's collapse is said to have destroyed him. In his last act in the theatre, Jewett brought a rope into the trap space beneath the stage and hanged himself.

He may have been ready to leave the world of the living, but apparently wasn't ready to leave his theatre. According to Sam Baltrusis in the book *Ghosts of Boston*, Jewett has continued to appear well into the twenty-first century, as a "larger than life" figure seated in the back of the orchestra section. Lights flicker for no reason and when the phones ring in the theatre offices, workers pick up to find a dead line. He is seen so frequently by the theatre's workers that he has acquired the nickname "Hank."

Jewett may bear yet another moniker, according to Holly Nadler's *Ghosts of Boston Town*. A "grainy, black apparition" called the Sentry has been seen patrolling the halls of the same theatre. Though frightening on first encounter, the Sentry is regarded by employees as a protective figure (like many theatre ghosts), making sure the theatre is safe from intruders.

To complete Jewett's eerie presence in the theatre, a painting of the theatre's founder hangs in the lobby today, costumed for the title role of Shakespeare's "cursed" play *Macbeth*.

VICTORIA THEATRE, DAYTON, OHIO

The Victoria Theatre in Dayton, Ohio, has a ghost—and a mystery. In the 1920s, an actress appearing there in a show went up to her dressing room to change her costume for her next scene. She locked the door from the inside . . . and was never seen or heard from again. The manager of the mansard-roofed theatre broke down the door, but there was no sign of where she might have gone, or how she got out of the windowless room. Subsequent actors who used that dressing room reported that when they looked into the makeup mirror they would sometimes see a woman's face staring back at them.

After the theatre was refurbished some years later, a strong smell of roses sometimes overcomes backstage folk, who have nicknamed the ghost Miss Vicky. The disembodied sound of rustling stiff material like taffeta also has been heard. These portents usually precede the apparition of a beautiful pale young women in a dark hallway or an otherwise unoccupied room.

And Miss Vicky isn't alone at the Victoria Theatre. Back in the nineteenth century a man chose the theatre as the scene of a particularly grisly suicide. Sitting in the auditorium, he jammed a knife handle into the seat in front of him, then impaled himself on the blade, soaking the carpeted floor of the theatre with his lifeblood which ran down the raked floor and dripped into the orchestra pit.

People have reported seeing his contorted face in the folds of the curtains shrouding the house-left exit door.

BAY STREET THEATRE, EUSTIS, FLORIDA.

At 109 North Bay Street in Eustis, Florida, sits a trim brick building with roll-up awnings, home of the Bay Street Players. It's a friendly-looking little playhouse, not the sort of place where you would expect to encounter the darker side of the other side.

The people who work there say the place is bubbling with paranormal activity—cold spots or an overwhelming sense of dread that seems to radiate from the walls in certain spots, especially the trap beneath the stage, known as "The Hole." There are no records of untimely deaths, as at so many other theatres, but encounters with spirits there are often chilling. Screaming sometimes issues from behind the locked door of the upstairs costume shop, and strangely lit orbs have been seen floating across the room. One night, early arriving audience members entered the balcony to see a man hanging by the neck from a hole in the ceiling. When they hysterically summoned the management, they found the hanged man had disappeared. More than once at tech rehearsals, the lighting and sound boards have acquired a life of their own, flashing the building's lights in a heartbeat rhythm.

Several employees reported trying an EVP (Electronic Voice Phenomenon) test on the stage and hearing frightening voices on their recording. One said he was told to leave and then was mysteriously scratched during one of these sessions. Whatever their origins, the ghosts at the Bay Street Players don't seem very happy.

FLORIDA THEATRE, JACKSONVILLE, FLORIDA

Another theatre in the Sunshine State, the aptly named Florida Theatre in Jacksonville, is very accommodating to its ghost. As part of a $10 million refurbishment of the 1927 playhouse, the theatre is replacing all 1,950 of its old seats, selling more than five hundred of them to the theatre's supporters and fans. But two upper-balcony seats, E1 and E2, are being carefully restored and returned to their original place. The seats are said to be haunted by the ghost of Joseph Hilton, onetime organist for the playhouse in its early days, who is believed to have committed suicide and now returns to watch and listen to the latest shows. He has been seen as a figure sitting in one of the seats or as a shadow moving around the balcony.

"We did not want our ghost to be homeless if his or her seat went away permanently," Numa Saisselin, president of the theatre, told the *Florida Times Union* in summer 2020. "They are the only two seats being restored. Every other seat is being replaced. Hopefully, the ghost does not mind being without his or her seat for a few weeks."

LINCOLN THEATRE, DECATUR, ILLINOIS

A stage hand known as One-Armed Red is said to have earned his grisly nickname in a fall from a catwalk to the stage at the Lincoln Theatre, tearing off one of his arms in the process. He lived just long enough to promise that he would return—and he has.

During his years working at the Lincoln in the 1920s prime of the vaudeville era, he was known just as "Red" for his brownish-red hair. He was renowned for "working high," which means something very different today. In those days it was a theatrical term for someone who had no fear of heights and was always available to climb the highest ladders to adjust a piece of scenery or change a lightbulb near the top of the "fly space." That's the tall hump you see at the backs of theatres where scenery can be hoisted high above the stage on ropes, which is termed "flying" the scenery.

Troy Taylor, in his history of the theatre, tells the story that this shy, theatre-loving craftsman was working "high" on a metal catwalk when he lost his balance and fell, catching his arm on a "pin rail," a rack with a series of steel hooks to which the ropes for the scenery were attached. As the legend goes, he caught his arm on one of these hooks as he fell, ripping off the arm, and died of shock and blood loss after slamming into the stage.

Taylor also says this colorful story, repeated in all its gory detail by generations of Illinois theatre folk, is just a fable. The real Red existed all right, but lost his arm in World War I, and, being stagestruck, worked at the theatre for nearly a decade, earning a reputation as someone who could do more work with a single arm than most other "hands" could do with two.

But here, reality veers back into supernatural territory. Red did die indeed at the theatre, but passed peacefully while napping after lunch at the theatre in 1927. Soon afterward, people began seeing a mysterious figure in various parts of the theatre, especially a spiral metal staircase backstage which he ascends and descends, scaring the pants off of unwary visitors. People who knew Red assumed this spirit was his, and the legend was born.

And Red apparently isn't alone at the Lincoln Theatre. The specter of a woman in a flowing period dress has been spotted in the balcony. There people have reported disembodied footsteps, mysterious whispers, voices you can hear (but not make out words), and movements out of the corner of their eyes.

Taylor himself reports more than one ghostly encounter at the Lincoln: "I was working in the quiet theatre one afternoon, making preparations for an upcoming Halloween show. I happened to be off to the side of the stage, behind some curtains, when I clearly heard someone walk up the steps and out onto the wooden stage. When I came out from behind the curtain, I was startled to find that there was no one there but me! I quickly searched the area, and even the rest of the theatre, but the place was completely empty."

Taylor also experienced the haunted spiral staircase—while in the company of a news reporter: "I was in the theatre one evening in

October 1995 with a reporter and a cameraman from a local television station. They had contacted me about haunted places in Central Illinois for a news special and one of the places that I took them to was the Lincoln Theatre. After an interview about the hauntings, I decided to join the cameraman, Robert Buchwald, for a trip up the spiral staircase. He took his camera along, hoping to film the theatre's stage from this vantage point. It was a good thing that he brought it, because we would have had no other source of light to make the trip up there with. We rounded the staircase and then reached the top. We looked around the small and confined space for a few moments, exploring a small room that leads to the theatre air ducts. . . .We had climbed the spiral staircase and left the reporter down on the stage by herself. We weren't surprised to soon hear the sound of her footsteps as she followed us up the stairs. Her hard-soled shoes made a distinctive sound as they echoed on the metal steps. Realizing that we had the only portable light, and the staircase was quite dark, Robert leaned over the railing with the camera so that the reporter would have some light to see by. Just as he did this, from out on the stage, we heard the sound of a voice calling out to us. We looked and saw the reporter standing in the middle of the stage— dozens of feet from the base of the steps and much too far away to have been climbing the staircase just moments before!"

AVON THEATRE, DECATUR, ILLINOIS

Red even has neighbors. At least a half-dozen ghosts are said to reside in the nearby Avon Theatre, reputed to be one of the most extensively haunted theatres in the United States outside New York. Laughter, applause, and voices can be heard in the empty orchestra long after the audience has departed for the night. Fifteen people who thought they'd have a hoot and went for a "ghost hunt" in the late 1990s collectively encountered a ghost believed to be former manager, Gus "Constan" Constanopoulos, who greeted them and dematerialized.

The Constanopoulos family owned the theatre from the 1920s until 1966, when it was bought by a chain of movie theatres. According to legend, Constan was so unhappy about the sale that he refused to leave his office and eventually had to be thrown out bodily onto North Water Street by agents of the new owners. The theatre's own official history reports that after Constan's death, "The [new] theatre manager, and the rest of the staff, reported that things . . . started to turn up missing in the theatre, both small items and large. They also told of hearing footsteps, laughter, applause, and voices coming from the auditorium after it had emptied for the night. The sounds of people walking about in empty rooms and in hallways were common, as was the feeling of being watched and being touched by ghostly hands. One staff member even claimed to have been groped by an invisible entity while working in the projection booth."

Among the hotspots creeping out employees to this day is the upstairs hallway where the theatre offices and a bathroom are located. Skip Huston, who later became the Avon's operator, was alone in one of the offices on a stormy afternoon when he heard a sound like footsteps behind him. He turned and checked the hallway but saw nothing. Minutes later he heard another noise and turned. "A man stood in the doorway to the room," Huston is quoted saying. "My first thought was that someone else was in the theatre, perhaps a homeless person hiding out there. He was of medium height and slender build. His age appeared to be in his late '50s or early '60s. His hair was close-cropped gray and black. He was not transparent or wraith-like. He appeared solid. His face was nondescript and he stared into the room, not looking at me, just staring. I started to speak to him and then he slowly turned and started down the hallway. Recovered from my surprise, I darted to the doorway to say something but all that I saw was an empty hall."

The same figure accommodatingly reappeared a few years later while Huston was conducting a ghost tour at the theatre. Fifteen or so others on the tour saw the figure, too, glaring down at them from the balcony.

They fled the theatre.

WESTPORT COUNTRY PLAYHOUSE, WESTPORT, CONNECTICUT

Westport Country Playhouse in Westport, Connecticut, is one of the oldest and most classic of "summer stock" theatres, having been founded in 1931 by New York producer Lawrence Langner. Countless current and future stage and film stars passed through its stage doors and across its boards, including composer Stephen Sondheim, who served as an apprentice there in 1950, just after graduating from Williams College.

The theatre is said to be filled with ghosts, but onetime wardrobe supervisor Randall Blair shared this story of his encounter with one he calls "The Man in the Balcony."

> My encounters with the "ghost" occurred during the years 1998–2003 and you need to understand the layout of the old Playhouse vs. the new. In the old Playhouse, the greenroom, wardrobe, and dressing rooms were all directly beneath the stage. The dressing rooms surrounded the greenroom and to

get to the stage there were two stairways. The stage left stair went up to house level and there was a door that led directly into house right by the front row, then the stairs turned and went up about four steps to stage left level. In the house area, there were doors on each side that opened directly to outdoors, which were sometimes opened when the air conditioning went out.

I usually stayed after performances and did laundry and prep for the next day's performance and it was not uncommon to hear creaks and other sounds coming from up onstage.

One evening as I was going about my duties, I kept hearing footsteps coming from up the stairs and what I thought was the passdoor shutting. I yelled out to see if some of the other crew were still in the building but got no response. I dismissed it and went on about my duties and then heard it again. I then thought I'd better go check to see if someone left a side door open and someone was wandering about. I went up to the stair landing that led into the house and the lock was in place to keep the audience members from using the door. I then went on up to stage level and ventured out onto the stage using the light from the "ghost" light . . . looking to see if someone was in the house area. I noticed a bit of movement coming from the balcony area on the house right side and as I held my hand above my eyes to shield the light coming from onstage, I thought I saw a faint image of a man sitting in the balcony.

I yelled, "Can I help you?" but got no response, shifted position, and started to repeat my question but the form/shape had disappeared. I shook it off and went back downstairs to close for the night.

This happened on several more occasions and as I became intrigued that this might actually be a theatre ghost, I decided to explore the possibility. One evening, I sat on the edge of the stage when the form was apparent just staring at the stage and began talking to it for some signal of who it might be. Never got a response other than the form would rise and appear to pace back and forth a bit, then sit again. Based on the history of the "barn," I always wondered if it was a worker from the tannery days who may have had an accident, or a theatrical person related to the early days of the Playhouse being established. The form was never clear enough to establish type of clothing but did seem to be male. The Playhouse was then renovated and reconfigured and in that first season of the new Playhouse (2005), I never felt that presence again.

CAPITOL THEATRE, WILLIMANTIC, CONNECTICUT

Theatre ghosts seem to have a special affinity for Connecticut. Ghosts have been reported at Nutmeg State theatres in Bridgeport, New Haven, and Hartford. But the Capitol Theatre at 896 Main Street in Willimantic is in its own category of haunted. The theatre opened in 1926 as a vaudeville house, but quickly switched to a combined bill of live acts and movies. It eventually became a full-time cinema but the years took their toll and it eventually began to crumble. The Capitol finally locked its doors in 1973 and sat moldering for three decades in the downtown of the state's rural northeast.

A $17 million renewal completed in 2002 restored the theatre's original Art Deco beauty and gave it new life as a regional arts magnet high school: Arts at the Capitol Theater (ACT). That's the backdrop for the hauntings that the new tenants have experienced. The students call them the "ACT Ghosts." Translucent wraiths have been spotted in the balcony, the catwalks, and in the dressing rooms. Disembodied voices, footsteps, and the crying of a child are also heard, with no apparent source. One of the voices appears to be an elderly woman who calls out for someone named Mary.

The theatre is said to have experienced two abrupt deaths in the 1920s that may have produced ghosts. In one, an actor was accidentally killed during a sword fight that turned real on the stage. In the other, a woman was shot to death by her jealous boyfriend who caught her with a lover in the balcony and hit her with a bullet meant for the other man. There is no hard record of such a murder, though there was a very similar love-triangle murder that took place at a dress shop next door.

Whatever the source, these spirits continue to give Willimantic the willies.

WOODSTOCK OPERA HOUSE IN WOODSTOCK, ILLINOIS

The box office at the Woodstock Opera House never sells the balcony seat DD-113. It is the favored spot of Elvira, a beautiful blonde female ghost who sometimes appears during rehearsals to boo, sigh, or make banging noises when she doesn't like what she sees.

Elvira, as she was dubbed by the Woodstock staff, possibly after a character in the play *Blithe Spirit* (see chapter 13), has a sad story, dating from a century ago. An aspiring ballet dancer, she reportedly pinned all her hopes on winning a particular role. Her audition didn't go as well as she had hoped and she was not chosen. In a paroxysm of youthful anger and disappointment, she is said to have climbed five stories to the bell tower on the beige and red brick building, threw herself off, and fell to her death.

Passersby on the street have spotted her peering out of the building's upper windows.

Workers at the theatre have glimpsed a nebulous figure with waist-length blonde hair and dressed in a filmy dance skirt. More often, she indulges in invisible mischief such as filching props and hiding them in odd places, or unfastening flats on sets so they collapse at unexpected moments.

People working on the stage have noticed the aforementioned balcony seat DD-113 in the "down" position, which is strange since the seats are spring-loaded and are designed stay in the "up" position when no one is sitting in them. When the workers go upstairs to check, the seat is always restored to its correct "up" position.

There is a sinister side to Elvira as well. Jealous of living young actresses, she will sometimes possess those who have just auditioned, put them in a trance, and try to lure them up to the bell tower. The theatre reportedly employs assistants to steer the young singers away from the stairs leading up.

Elvira's efforts to win herself some otherworldly company have consistently failed—so far.

ORPHEUM THEATRE, MEMPHIS, TENNESSEE

The Orpheum Theatre at 203 S. Main Street in Memphis is inhabited by the ghost of Mary, a sweet twelve-year-old who took up residence in a previous theatre that stood on the same spot in the early 1920s. The current Orpheum was built in 1928 and Mary seems to have stuck around to enjoy it.

Musician Vincent Astor has taken on the mantle of Orpheum Theatre historian, and he's especially interested in Mary, and several other ghosts that have colonized the old playhouse.

Astor said his first encounter with Mary came

when I had some friends down after a show we had closed that night at Circuit Playhouse. I brought [these] friends down [to the Orpheum] to play the organ for them. And somebody said, "Who's that?" They saw a little girl in white playing in the lobby. [These were] people that I trusted and people that were not under the influence of any controlled substance. So we began to wonder. We'd heard tales about a little girl [ghost] that had been seen in the theatre. . . . [She] was described as a girl about twelve years old with long dark braids in a white short dress with black stockings but no shoes. We figured the reason for that was that she wasn't buried with shoes on because shoes were expensive.

And people started seeing her when I would play quiet music, especially children's songs like "Never Never Land" [from the musical *Peter Pan*, which] seemed to be her very favorite.

She'd been seen here, there and yonder, but most often in the Grand Loge [seating section] on the north side, the third row, the seat closest to the railing, which in those days was Row 3 Seat 5. . . .

[As for the source of the name "Mary,"] people have called her everything and I'm not going to tell you a bunch of the silly things she's been called. But in the early '70s we had a parapsychology professor from the University of Memphis come to investigate: Dr. Lee Sutter. He brought his class down here . . . and I played the organ. Then we set up a ouija board—right here on stage not far from where I'm sitting—to see what would happen. That's where we started hearing about the year 1921 and the name Mary. . . .

[The ghost of] Mary had been accused of laughing, crying, moving tools in the organ chambers for someone who is working on the organ, sneaking around, and, of course, scaring the daylights out of people. I had a person down here who had nerves of steel and was re-lamping the dome for me, which is a bit treacherous. He didn't believe in ghosts. I was playing the organ before we got started, and he and Mary were playing hide and go seek around the post up in the loge!

Buddy Kirkland told me the story about the tools being moved around by someone who wasn't there 'cause he was all alone in the organ chamber. An usher told me . . . that one night the mezzanine was closed. The main floor is so big, they only opened upstairs when it was really, really busy. He saw this little girl sitting up in the mezzanine. He went up the back stairs into the loge to tell her to come downstairs. He didn't find the little girl; he found a [live] young woman who had walked up there and was eating her lunch while she was watching the movie. They fell in love, and it was all Mary's doing!

[In] the very first production of [the Broadway musical] *Annie* that came through here, the girl playing Annie was . . . named Rosanne Sorrentino. There's this scene where Annie escapes from the orphanage [by hiding] in a big laundry basket. [Sorrentino] was in the laundry basket and someone spoke to her one night that she thinks was Mary.

Anything that has manifested in this theatre has usually been seen when it was quiet . . . [and] most of the time when people are not looking very hard. If someone comes to the theatre and they feel a sort of a strange, icky feeling in the balcony? Just move away. If they see a little girl in white on the mezzanine, just wonder, because all she's doing is watching the show. It's very special if you see the little girl in white because she can be very shy and she doesn't turn up on cue.

There are as many as seven different feelings or spirits or something . . . in this theatre. Mary is the most famous, but there is another, a male spirit that is white and luminous. . . . It was conjectured that he was a guide that was going to take [Mary] across [to the afterlife]. Some people have called him David. But [the ghost of Mary] was wary of him and wouldn't go near him. So he is stuck here as long as she stays here.

There's a very unhappy woman [ghost] in the balcony, in the foyer. One of the people that visited here said her name was Eleanor and that she died in the '30s. She [had been] jilted and was just very, very unhappy.

A bad experience that I had way, way back before I knew about any of this, was [getting] that weird cold feeling [in the balcony]. It feels like you just put your hand into a tub full of raw liver! Can you imagine that? It's slick and it's cold and it's eerie and it happened to me in the balcony. And I bolted. I think now that was the spirit called Eleanor. She's very, very unhappy and people that run across her . . . have this unhappy, icky feeling. It's not malevolent, like she's going to make something happen, or she's going to "get you" or something. It's just this real I-don't-want-to-be-here [sensation] and she, for some reason, can't leave either.

MAJESTIC THEATRE IN BOSTON, MASSACHUSETTS

We've looked at the phenomenon of "friendly" theatre ghosts. But Boston seems to be home to more than its share of the other variety.

Boston's gorgeous old Majestic Theatre, now owned by Emerson College, was built in 1903 to house opera productions. After it was acquired by the burgeoning Shubert Organization, it showcased both distinguished legitimate theatre and vaudeville well into the 1920s. After that, the great playhouse's gentle but inexorable decline continued, following much the same route as New York's 42nd Street theatres, switching to showing mainstream movies, then "action" films, and, finally, cheap adult movies. The theatre's original Beaux Arts interior was damaged by a series of midcentury renovations.

It didn't help that the theatre was located in the neighborhood that came to be known as the "Combat Zone," owing to the prevalence of prostitution and drug-dealing. The area has improved substantially in recent years, but the spirits of the proud old playhouse seem to have been unhappy with the dark era, especially in the blue-nosed city that lent its name to the expression "Banned in Boston."

The theatre was acquired by Emerson in 1983 and enjoyed a far more respectful full renovation in 2003, sponsored by Ted and Joan Benard-Cutler, which led to the building's renaming as the Emerson Cutler Majestic Theatre. These changes may have helped to awaken some of the spirits frequently seen or experienced there today.

The Majestic has been designated a Boston Historical Landmark and is operated as a professional legitimate resident theatre and a training ground for Emerson theatre students. Recent offerings include Broadway musicals, dance companies, and original plays.

A well-dressed spirit frequently seen by staff throughout the theatre is called the Mayor, because legend tells that a onetime Boston mayor died in the theatre during a performance. I could find no record of such an occurrence to any public official of any kind in the building, but that is how he continues to be known. Nevertheless, a tuxedoed figure with an old-fashioned hairstyle has been seen prowling about, or just standing and watching the stage. Sometimes he turns and looks at the person who sees him—and slowly dematerializes.

A tragic car accident seems to have led to the theatre's haunting by a sad family of ghosts. A father, a mother, and their young daughter were reportedly killed together in a car crash as they were leaving the theatre after an evening's performance. The young couple sometimes appear as fully articulated living beings who sit in seats and even speak to other patrons sitting near them in the balcony section, but then mysteriously vanish before intermission without being seen to rise and depart.

The child manifests in a much more heartbreaking way. She is sometimes seen—but more frequently heard—alone and crying. Staffers and student interns who have heard the crying have searched the theatre for its source, but can never find her.

The balcony where the ghostly couple is seen was closed off due to fire regulations for many years, but it was reopened after the 2003 renovation, leading to a fresh round of sightings. The balcony is also reportedly a favorite haunt of the Mayor, possibly seeking votes from the couple.

But one room, a former dressing room, remains closed off, and for good reason. Known as the "Nightmare Room," the space is said to be the most haunted spot in the Majestic. There are no ghostly sightings, but those who have entered the room report a powerful sense of unease and difficulty breathing, and sometimes even the acute sensation of being touched by ghostly hands. They feel they are being watched by a powerfully malevolent presence, and will sometimes whirl about to see who is there, only to find themselves alone—and terrified.

SOMERVILLE THEATRE, SOMERVILLE, MASSACHUSETTS

Just outside Boston in the community of Somerville, the Somerville Theatre, one of the area's few remaining independent cinemas, houses a spirit that seems to have been leftover from its days as a repertory theatre and vaudeville house.

Manager Ian Judge said the theatre has two haunted seats, J1 and J2, in the orchestra section. These are the old-fashioned seats that can be flipped up to allow theatregoers to sidle in an out of the rows. Judge said employees would flip up all the seats after the last showing each night, but then find J1 and J2 flipped down again the next day. Staffers who stayed to see what was causing the problem witnessed the seats flipping up and down on their own.

MISHLER THEATRE, ALTOONA, PENNSYLVANIA

Moving south now to central Pennsylvania, we come to a story told by actor Chris Tracy, who encountered a famous but unnamed ghost at the Mishler Theatre, located on the Altoona campus of Pennsylvania State University. "I was cast as Sky Masterson [in *Guys and Dolls*] at the Mishler, a famously haunted vaudeville house whose gas fittings could still be seen in their footlight bays. Throughout rehearsals a number of cast members (most notably our Sarah Brown, the wife of a local undertaker not known for magical thinking) described lights coming on and off or walking through cold spaces in an otherwise heated facility. On one occasion I thought I saw someone sitting in the empty balcony as I approached down center for 'Luck Be a Lady,' though when I looked back up a few seconds later there was no one there. My later discreet inquiries found no stagehand or visitor in the area at the time."

Tracy is not the only recipient of the Mishler ghosts' attention. In fact, many believe it is Mishler himself—Isaac "Doc" Mishler, who built the onetime vaudeville house in 1906 and then rebuilt it in 1907 when the first one burned to the ground just months after it opened. Mishler sunk every penny he had into that theatre, and ran it successfully for years, until the death of vaudeville slowed business down. He followed it in 1944. Having put his life into the playhouse, he has been putting his death into it, too.

Mishler appears as a man in period dress, smoking his signature cigar. Sometimes no figure appears, but the smell of cigar smoke gradually fills the air even if no one is smoking. Theatre workers have stories of seeing him appear in the wings, or in the balcony watching their activity, as happened to Tracy.

The creepiest but also kind of sweet story is told by Madeleine Letsche of Altoona, who visited the theatre with her mother when she was a child. She remembers wandering around its rooms and passageways alone and at will, while her mother, Laura, worked as a sound and lighting technician at the historic playhouse. Madeleine said that it was in those halls where she met a friendly man who wore a different funny hat each time she came. The friendly man would tour her around the theatre, extolling its history and beauty.

Mishler may have sold the theatre decades ago, but still retains a spirit of ownership.

DOCK STREET THEATRE, CHARLESTON, SOUTH CAROLINA

The 1809-vintage Dock Street Theatre, now standing on a site where a theatre operated as early as 1736, has an especially lurid ghost story. The current building was used for a time as a hotel called the Planters Inn. According to the theatre's historians, a local prostitute named Nettie Dickerson was standing on the balcony of the Inn when a bolt of lightning struck her and launched her into the next world. She apparently still haunts the building's second floor "crazy-eyed and dressed in a red gown," according to one account.

Her choice of attire also puts her into a special sisterhood of ghosts, the so-called "Ladies in Red" who haunt places from Chicago's Drake Hotel to the St. Anthony Hotel in San Antonio, Texas, to the Korakia Pensione in Palm Springs, California, to a dozen others around the United States. But Nettie is one of the few who have the good taste to haunt a hotel that was also a theatre. Red also happens to be the color many costume designers like to reserve for leading ladies, so she was, conveniently, perfectly costumed for the role of theatre ghost.

THE KENNEDY CENTER, WASHINGTON, DC

You've read of many kinds of ghosts: scary ghosts, helpful ghosts, flirtatious ghosts, melancholy ghosts, and many others. But my opinion, now, is that you've come to the most adorable of theatre ghosts: Mosby, the Kennedy Center cat.

This cat was already considered something of a ghost even while he was still alive. As the Kennedy Center was under construction in the late 1960s and early 1970s, workers would hear caterwauling coming from the site. Occasionally spotted and sometimes fed, the cat was dubbed Mosby, after John Singleton Mosby, a Confederate cavalry battalion commander who earned the nickname The Gray Ghost for his ability to slip in and out of the Union lines in the nearby Shenandoah Valley during the Civil War.

The Kennedy Center opened September 8, 1971, and Mosby, who retained his stray status despite being cared for by the staff, earned a reputation for sounding off during performances. Roger L. Stevens, chairman of the Kennedy Center from 1961 to 1988, recalled Mosby making sounds "not unlike the keening at an Irish wake" accompanying the foghorn sound effects during a production of Eugene O'Neill's mournful *Long Day's Journey into Night* with Zoe Caldwell and Jason Robards.

Mosby apparently mastered a repertoire of meows, because during a performance of the play *Finishing Touches* with Barbara Bel Geddes, he would imitate the sound of a baby crying. Author Beppie Noyes, who wrote a semi-fictional book about Mosby, records his "long, lonely howls" transmitted through ducts in the building. "The metal pipe echoed, rather like singing in a shower, giving his voice added depth. It sounded like a man he had heard in the Opera House."

Mosby's golden age lasted from 1971 to January 1977 when he suddenly disappeared on the night of Jimmy's Carter's inauguration. In her book, Noyes speculated that Mosby moved to the White House with the Carters, though there is no evidence that he did so. The date of his death is unknown.

Apparently nine lives weren't quite enough for Mosby. He gives evidence of happily living a tenth at the Kennedy Center. Performers report that a ghostly cat can be felt rubbing invisibly against their legs and issuing mews that seem to come from all directions at once.

This is one of the most beloved ghosts in any theatre—to the point where the Kennedy Center sells stuffed Mosby dolls in its gift shop.

As it turns out, Mosby is not the only feline ghost in Washington, DC. There is a much older and much more nightmarish cat stalking Pennsylvania Avenue. Capital workers have been reporting sightings of the Washington, DC, Demon Cat since the mid-nineteenth century. Originally part of a clowder released in the Capitol building to pounce on an infestation of rats and mice, the Demon Cat reportedly makes his home in the stately building's sub-basement, and appears to humans as a portent to major tragedies, such as the assassination of presidents, including both Abraham Lincoln and John F. Kennedy.

First appearing as a normal-size black kitty, the Demon Cat reportedly doesn't just bristle when confronted, but blossoms to the size of a tiger and chases humans. Capitol Hill guards are said to have fired pistols at it, and one even died of a heart attack after witnessing one of its materializations.

Hoping to piggyback on the ghost's reputation for ferocity, one of the city's amateur roller derby teams, the DC DemonCats, is named for it.

HAUNTED U.S. THEATRES OF THE WEST

Crossing the Mississippi, we come to the West, where there is no shortage of ghosts that have taken up residence in busy theatres. Most of the theatre ghosts in New York tend to haunt legitimate theatres, but the ghosts of Los Angeles naturally tend to have more cinematic connections.

PANTAGES THEATRE, LOS ANGELES

The ghost of reclusive movie mogul billionaire Howard Hughes (1905–1976; uncredited producer of two dozen Hollywood movies, including *The Front Page*, *Scarface*, and *Two Tickets to Broadway*, and himself the subject of the film *The Aviator*) reportedly haunts the business offices on the second floor of the Pantages Theatre in Los Angeles, which he once owned. He appears as a tall man standing in the office doorways, and rattles drawers in a second floor office.

And Hughes isn't alone at the Pantages. At least a dozen other spirits are said to stalk its halls. One is the theatre's namesake, producer Alexander Pantages. The other is a woman said to have died in the mezzanine in 1932. She has a special haunting style: the eerie sound of a female voice singing, as if from a great distance, which has been heard at various spots around the theatre.

LANCASTER PERFORMING ARTS CENTER, ANTELOPE VALLEY, CALIFORNIA

How do theatres acquire their ghosts? As we've seen, it's usually from someone dying at the theatre, or having such a close affinity over many years that their spirits become attached to the place. It's rare for such a new theatre to have a ghost already, but the Lancaster Performing Arts Center in Antelope Valley, California, is said to be haunted by an elderly woman named Viola who was taking a guided tour of the site when the building was being constructed in 1990. She reportedly was killed when she lost her footing and fell into the orchestra pit, then under construction—which she now haunts, along with the theatre's catwalks.

Viola appears to be a benevolent spirit, and has adjusted well to her new posthumous status. She creates disembodied footsteps and "odd noises." Speakers that have their power turned off still emit strange crackles of static.

A former employee, who wants to be identified as "Absinthe," said the entire staff "are rather proud of their 'resident spook,' and whenever anything odd happens or something goes missing, people will shake their heads and say, 'Well, there is Viola again!'"

PALACE THEATRE, LOS ANGELES, CALIFORNIA

There is another Palace Theatre beyond Broadway: it's clear over on the West Coast of the United States, and it, too, has a ghost. The Los Angeles Palace Theatre has stood at 630 South Broadway since 1911—predating the one in Times Square by two years.

It was built as the Orpheum Theatre to serve the City of Angels as a two-a-day (i.e., high class) vaudeville theatre on the Orpheum Circuit. In 1926, the Orpheum company built a bigger theatre just down the street (also said to be haunted) to serve the burgeoning population of L.A., and renamed the first theatre as the Broadway Palace, then under new ownership as the Fox Palace, later shortened to just the Palace. With the fade-out of vaudeville in the late 1920s, the Palace became a cinema, showcasing the movies made just a few miles away in Hollywood.

Originally built with two balconies, the Palace found that moviegoers didn't like sitting up so high. The second balcony was closed in 1930 and has remained unused ever since—at least by the living.

Actors working on the stage say they see shadowy figures moving up there—which they shouldn't because the door is sealed. Meanwhile, on the stage itself, a woman in an old-fashioned lacy gown has been seen coming out to center stage, then melting into the shadows in the wings.

The Palace continued as a cinema until 2000, when new owners refurbished it as a rental house, showcasing touring theatre shows and concerts.

The theatre found a way to moonlight in the late twentieth century, not with the movies it showed, but with the movies it was in. The Palace was used as a location for films that have scenes in and near theatres, including *Dreamgirls, The Big Lebowski, El Norte, Mikey and Nicky, Mulholland Drive, The Hidden,* as a concert hall for the "My Boy Friend's Back" number in the film of *Jersey Boys,* and as a stand-in for an old Burlesque theatre in 1993 TV movie version of *Gypsy* with Bette Midler.

The Palace may have reached the zenith of its fame as a theatre playing a theatre in Michael Jackson's 1983 music video of the title track from the *Thriller* album, which shows Jackson dancing menacingly with a swarm of zombies. With all those "undead" running around, the ghosts of the L.A. Palace must have felt right at home.

HOLLYWOOD PACIFIC THEATRE, HOLLYWOOD, CALIFORNIA

The Hollywood Pacific Theatre at 6433 Hollywood Boulevard in Hollywood couldn't possibly get any more "movie land" than it does with an address like that. But it almost didn't open at all.

Sam Warner of Warner Brothers fought an epic financial battle—a lot of it with his brothers—trying to build a palatial 2,700-seat movie mecca to showcase the new "talkie" film format he was developing in the 1920s. The first commercially released sound film, *The Jazz Singer,* caused a sensation when it was released in 1927. And the theatre finally opened in 1928 with the movie *Glorious Betty,* but Sam wasn't around to see either of them, having died one day before *The Jazz Singer's* release in 1927.

The theatre's ups and downs continued over the ensuing decades until it closed in 1994 due to water damage cause by some nearby construction. Those who have worked at the theatre say they sometimes run into Sam Warner's ghost wandering through the halls of the theatre he worked so hard to bring into being, and they blame him when personal items go missing, only to reappear days later someplace far from where they were placed. The ghost was also seen riding the elevator in the theatre.

SACRAMENTO THEATRE COMPANY, SACRAMENTO, CALIFORNIA,

So much paranormal activity has been reported at the Sacramento Theatre Company in Sacramento, California, that the space has been systematically studied by several psychics and at least one medium who held a séance in the space trying to contact any of a half dozen spirits said to reside there.

They're especially interested in whatever entity is behind the pink aura that surrounds a ghost the staff has dubbed Pinky, believed to be a former stagehand. They don't want to scare Pinky away, however. The ghost was credited with warning electricians about the imminent collapse of an overhead lighting bar, and helping an actress find a lost lipstick. Among the other spirits is Joan the Seamstress, who haunts the costume shop, moving spools of thread around and running a sewing machine when the room is empty.

BRADY THEATRE, TULSA, OKLAHOMA

The great operatic tenor Enrico Caruso once rang the rafters in the most prestigious halls of Europe and America: La Scala in Milan, the

Royal Opera House, in London, the Metropolitan Opera in New York, and the Mariinsky Theatre in Saint Petersburg.

So why would he haunt the Brady Theatre on Brady Street in Tulsa? Maybe he liked the dry climate and the friendly—if slightly confused at his presence—people. After all, these are the descendants of the likes of Curley, Laurie, and the other settlers of Oklahoma we know from the musical of the same name.

Whatever the reason, those who spend time at the Brady and have experienced his supernatural visits say that, yes, it's Caruso.

So, again, why the Brady? It turns out that the "The Old Lady on Brady," as its fans have dubbed the 4,200-seat theatre, is one of the last places the tenor performed before his death. While some ghosts are free to wander, most ghosts seem to become locked into the place where they died or contracted their fatal illness. Maybe Caruso is just afraid this is the closest to heaven he's going to get.

Bill Underwood of *Tulsa World* interviewed theatre owner Peter Mayo about how it happened: "Local promoters who were producing Caruso's concert wanted to take him out to an oil field the day of the show. Caruso agreed, but on the way, their car broke down on a lonely dirt road. 'He already had a history of lung problems and this was a cold, blustery day in Oklahoma,' Mayo said. 'So they were out there trying to hitch a ride back for three or four hours.' Eventually, the men were rescued and Caruso gave his performance that evening at the Brady. From all accounts it was one of his better shows. Then, six to eight months later, the opera star died of lung complications in another American city [actually Naples, Italy]. Since that time, locals like to say that it was the cold weather out at the oil field that resulted in Caruso's death. And, as a result, the legendary singer's ghost comes back to the Brady from time to time just to haunt the theatre."

CENTENNIAL HALL AT THE UNIVERSITY OF ARIZONA, TUCSON, ARIZONA

Talk about good cop/bad cop, Centennial Hall at the University of Arizona in Tucson boasts a pair of specters. One, a woman in a long white Victorian-style dress, haunts the upper balcony and appears primarily during classical music concerts. She is said to have tripped people going up and down the steps, and shoved visitors walking down hallways.

Her mischief is countered by the theatre's other ghost, a Spanish man dressed in black who tries to help those she has harmed. Perhaps he is trying to make up for losing his life in a duel with another man over a woman they both desired.

This complementary pair of specters are two of at least a half a dozen ghosts said to haunt various spots on the U of A campus.

RIALTO THEATRE IN SOUTH PASADENA, CALIFORNIA

Most theatres have no worries from ghosts—neither man, woman, nor beast. But the Spanish Baroque masterpiece that is the 1925 vintage Rialto Theatre on Route 66 in South Pasadena, California, has all three.

The Rialto was the scene of a horrific suicide in the 1930s. A girl crept up to the empty ladies room and slit her wrists, eventually making her bloody way to the balcony and bleeding to death before she was found. Perhaps the punishment for this crime against herself is to stay trapped inside the building for eternity. Like Moaning Myrtle in the

Harry Potter books, she haunts the ladies' bathroom, sometimes to be heard shrieking and shaking the doors on the stalls, terrifying women using the facilities.

And she's not alone. A man is said to have gone insane in the projectionist's booth of this onetime home for midnight showings of the cult film *The Rocky Horror Picture Show*. A shadowy male figure is still sometimes seen on the steps in the same balcony where the female suicide breathed her last.

The two human ghosts are also said to share the theatre with the ghost of a cat who had been something of a mascot to the workers there, and the feline was allowed to roam the house freely including the stage, even during screenings of films. His small shadow can still sometimes be seen moving around the audience space, and when this feline apparition crosses in front of the screen, an "eerie red light" marks its passage.

The theatre *itself* is a ghost of a kind. Originally built to house vaudeville, the Rialto soldiered on after that art form died. It rose again and was rebuilt after two devastating fires, and after the bankruptcy of various owners over the years. Thanks to a landmarking designation, it fended off demolition and continues to stand. Listed on the National Register of Historic Places, it's now the Mosaic Church. One hopes the ministers there may be able to help the spirits to find their way to a happier afterlife.

The theatre had one moment of recent glory: it was used for a location shoot in the Oscar-nominated film *La La Land* in the scene where Sebastian takes Mia to see the movie *Rebel without a Cause* on their first date.

MACKY AUDITORIUM CONCERT HALL, BOULDER, COLORADO

Macky Auditorium Concert Hall stands on the hillside campus of the University of Colorado in Boulder. The theatre was named for Andrew J. Macky, a successful Boulder banker who died in 1907, leaving $300,000 for the construction of an auditorium, a lasting gift to the town that had given him so much.

But Macky's daughter contested the will, which wound up in probate for more than a decade. The theatre was finally completed in 1921, boasting a pair of distinctively crenellated towers, and hosting visits from the likes of composer John Phillip Sousa, author Helen Keller, and poet Robert Frost to help enrich the education of the locals and the students. In 1985 the building became a concert hall, hosting, over the years, performances by the likes of Judy Collins, George Carlin, James Taylor, Neil Young, Dave Matthews, and Tori Amos.

The beauty and renown of the setting may have been a factor that drew young Elaura Jaquette to study opera at the university in the 1960s. And it was in one of those famous crenellated towers in July 1966 that Jaquette was bludgeoned, raped, and murdered while using the space to rehearse. She didn't go easily. A cover story in the *Daily Sentinel* of Grand Junction, Colorado, cites a "fatal struggle" leading to the death. A janitor was found to be guilty of the crime, but poor Jaquette, who just wanted to sing, apparently continues to do so long after death. Late at night, after the building is closed, passersby have heard loud opera music playing, or a *Phantom of the Opera*–like organ running up and down the scales with no one in the building, and a high-pitched voice wailing an accompaniment. The wispy form of a young woman has been spotted wafting through the tower's hallways. Bloodstains are said to appear on the walls and floor of the room where the murder is alleged to have taken place, now a professor's office.

But why shouldn't Jaquette still have a chance at an opera career? There are many female ghosts in opera that might be perfect for her: Liza in *Queen of Spades*, Marie in *Die Todt Stadt*, Marie Antoinette in *The Ghosts of Versailles*, and others. She's certainly been keeping up with her rehearsals.

DOLE CANNERY SIGNATURE THEATRE, HONOLULU, HAWAII

This ghost was tough to pin down. All available published accounts have basically the same tidbits of information, and even these are hard to confirm. But there is something compelling about the story. And the number of similar reports lends credence to the legend, or at least makes you wonder exactly what may be going on there.

The Dole Food Company, known especially for its pineapple, grown mainly in Hawaii where it was founded, is now headquartered in Ireland. But for many years the company owned farms and processing plants throughout the Hawaiian Islands, and operated a cannery at 735 B Iwilei Road, Honolulu, on the island of Oahu. The cannery is reputed to have been built over a *luakini heiau,* in the Hawaiian native religion, a walled and paved place to worship.

The cannery closed and the building was converted in 2002 to an entertainment complex, including stores, restaurants, and a multiplex movie theatre, now formally known as the Regal Dole Cannery

ScreenX, welcoming modern audiences through a green metal frame entryway.

But back in the cannery days of the 1980s, something terrible apparently happened there. A bus carrying schoolchildren lost control and crashed into the building, resulting in the deaths of some of its young passengers. Afterward, the building was reportedly plagued with the wails of children, and visited by a glum older male ghost, believed to have been a cannery worker, or perhaps the bus driver, who also paid for the accident with his life.

The cannery may have been gutted and refurbished as a modern mall, but that doesn't seem to have displaced these ghosts, all of whom appear to have taken up residence in the cinema. The crying and screaming children have been heard in the restroom next to the screening space. The older man now appears in the last row corner in screening room 14. He presents as a nonthreatening lone figure who will materialize during movies, gazing out over the audience, then disappearing.

Although reports of the ghosts are fairly widespread, especially in social media, I could find no documentary evidence of a such a bus accident in the time frame often cited. The accident story may have been conjured up to account for the sound of screaming children, but the sound appears to be something genuinely heard by many.

ROSELAND THEATER, PORTLAND, OREGON

For years, the January 23, 1990, killing of twenty-one-year-old Roseland Theater promoter Tim Moreau stood as one of the great unsolved murders in the trendy city of Portland. But thanks to tireless investigative journalism from reporter Jim Redden in *Willamette Week* and more recently in the *Portland Tribune*, blame for the murder came to rest on Larry Hurwitz. Hurwitz was the owner of the 1922 vintage theatre, formerly the Apostolic Faith Church, which he turned into a rock concert venue renamed Starry Night. In renovating the building, Hurwitz removed a neon sign on the church that had become a local landmark: "Jesus, the Light of the World."

Redden unearthed evidence that Hurwitz had murdered Moreau when he discovered Hurwitz was running a counterfeit ticket scam, overbooking the theatre and failing to report income. Hurwitz responded by slapping Redden and *Willamette Week* with a $5 million libel suit. It backfired. During the discovery phase of the trial, further evidence came to light that eventually led to Hurwitz's conviction on murder charges in 2000. George Castagnola, one of Hurwitz' business associates, eventually told the authorities that he had held Moreau down while Hurwitz strangled him in the backstage hallway of Starry Night. Moreau's corpse was sneaked out of the building and reportedly buried at an unknown location in the Columbia River Gorge, a twenty-minute drive from the theatre. Moreau's body has never been found, despite several focused recovery efforts.

Aside from the lurid details of the murder, one of the factors spurring public interest in the cast was the fact that soon after the killing, the red and white brick theatre located at 8 Northwest Sixth Avenue in the Old Town Chinatown neighborhood started to practically shake with paranormal incidents. Items were moved, icy spots were felt backstage, and "angry whispers" were often heard in the theatre's passageways. Sometimes an icy blast hit the audience, not caused by air conditioning. Worst of all, patrons reported feeling a burning, choking sensation around their necks, with no apparent cause.

New owners have changed the name back to the Roseland Theater, and under that moniker it has resumed booking rock concerts, including the bands Theory of a Deadman, Can't Swim, City Morgue, and, in 2015, Ghost.

OPERA HOUSE THEATRE, PHILIPSBURG, MONTANA

From outside, the neat brick building at 140 South Sansome Street in Philipsburg might not strike you as looking like a theatre, but it was built as an opera house in 1891, switched to movies in the 1920s, and now hosts live performances all summer from its resident theatre company. It's the oldest continuously operating theatre in the state—and also reputed to be the most haunted.

The Opera House Theatre ghost (or ghosts) manifests in several ways. It is sometimes seen as a wispy, translucent figure, or experienced as an unaccountably ice-cold spot.

People who enter the building, even after it has been empty overnight, are confronted with the smell of a freshly smoked cigar. This mischievous revenant also has a penchant for yanking the hair of audience members, even during performances.

CAPITOL THEATRE, SALT LAKE CITY, UTAH

A seventeen-year-old usher named Richard Duffin helped hundreds of audience members evacuate the Capitol Theatre in Salt Lake City,

Utah, when it caught fire during a matinee performance in 1949. But Duffin went back inside once too often and wound up succumbing to smoke inhalation in the theatre's basement. Workers at the theatre report lights turning on and off, unexplained banging noises, and a sudden pervasive reek of smoke. Moreover, people passing through the basement are sometimes overwhelmed with a feeling of anger that seems to come from outside themselves. If it indeed emanates from the spirit of the hero taken too young, who could blame him?

GUTHRIE THEATRE, MINNEAPOLIS, MINNESOTA

Mark Lamos, the distinguished two-time Tony Award–nominated stage director and administrator, has pursued most of his career on Broadway and at theatres in New England. While he was artistic director of Hartford State Company in Connecticut, the theatre won a special Tony Award as outstanding regional theatre. He is currently artistic director of the landmark Westport Country Playhouse, also in Connecticut.

Lamos says he has experienced no ghostly manifestations at either of those playhouses. But it was while he was performing at a midwestern theatre early in his career that he had his brushes with the supernatural.

As he tells it,

> One afternoon in the 1970s when I was an actor at the Guthrie Theatre in Minneapolis, I was resting in my dressing room between matinee and evening performances. In those days the theatre employed a live orchestra and the musicians were placed at the back of the stage, a few feet from my dressing room. As I was drifting off to sleep, I heard the playing of

a harp. Jangled notes, mostly, and a few glissandos. Anyone going to the orchestra space would have had to pass the open door of my dressing room in order to get to the instrument. I got up, but just as I walked through the door onto the stage, the music stopped, its last note vibrating in the stillness. I stood among empty orchestra seats. No one was there but me. After a moment, I turned and hurried upstairs to the green room. When I told some senior members of the acting company what had just happened, they clapped me on the back and told me I had just experienced "The Ghost."

The Guthrie Theatre ghost had been a young usher who'd died during the theatre's earliest seasons. Shortly after his funeral, audience members in Aisle 10 complained of a troublesome usher, one who hadn't shown them to their seats. People who'd been at the Guthrie for a few seasons told me that he roamed the theatre day and night.

Three years after the harp episode, I was rehearsing a role in *A Winter's Tale*, and the director asked me to choreograph some dances for it. The rehearsal halls were filled, so I was given time on the Guthrie stage. House lights illuminated the vast, empty 1,400-seat auditorium as I jumped about without inhibition, creating steps and movement, and racing periodically to the tape machine to rewind, start over, and jot down ideas onto paper. Just as I was luxuriating in the feeling that the theatre was completely mine, I turned and noticed a man sitting in the balcony, dead center, watching me. I waved and called hello. He didn't move or answer. He wore a uniform: beige coat, brown lapels. I felt a wave of animosity like a chilling breeze. I knew he was the Usher. I left the stage as quickly as I could manage.

About a month later, just after the play had opened, I was waiting with two actresses backstage in complete darkness for our cue to begin the second act. But just as it was called, both girls screamed, and I felt them jostle violently against me, as if they had been pushed. There was no time to think. We rushed onstage in the dark, pushing a large papier-mâché tree. They exited, leaving me in front of it as the lights came up. When the scene ended, I rushed off stage. Both women were sobbing uncontrollably. They'd been grabbed from behind, they said, physically attacked in that moment in the dark. There was no room where we'd been waiting for our cue. No one else could have fit into that tiny offstage space. The Usher, I thought. The actresses said they knew it was him.

Sometimes his manifestations were less wickedly playful, more aesthetically beautiful—but frightening, nonetheless, to mortal eyes. I remember a young night watchman who ran, white-faced and breathless, into the theatre's bar after a performance as a group of actors finished their drinks. He'd been making his rounds and had noticed a door ajar on the top floor of the theatre. When he opened the door he saw a radiant light flicker and move around a series of hanging props [and] chandeliers, causing crystals to tinkle gently. And of course, there was no human being in the room but the young watchman.

My last story happened during a dress rehearsal for Marlowe's *Doctor Faustus*, in which I was playing the title role. While technicians and designers fussed with the lighting cue, I waited nervously in the wings, suddenly overcome with a fear of failure. The Guthrie was taking a big chance on a relatively young actor, and Faustus was the largest role I'd ever played. As I stood fidgeting in the dark, I felt someone hug me. I turned to see who it was. No one was there. The hug continued nonetheless, and became a warm, generous embrace, filled with deep feeling. I felt cared for, loved. My fear vanished. Only one person in the world hugged me like that: my father, who had died suddenly while visiting me in Minneapolis less than a year before. After a few moments, the sweet pressure around my chest and shoulders softened, and I made my entrance onto the stage full of confidence, into the light.

Ghosts supposedly manifest not only the leftover energy of a life cut short but also, perhaps, the projections, neurosis, and visions of those who claim to experience their occasional surprising presence in our current lives. I prefer to think that it may be a combination of the two. A spiritual mathematic equation. A self-induced reality, but Theatre.

10

THE GHOSTS OF LONDON'S THEATRES

L ondon may be the most haunted city in the world. Ghost touring in the British capital is a small industry of its own, and many of the stops are at the West End's most popular theatres. The city has been home to theatre for the better part of six hundred years, plenty of time for generations of ghosts to take up residence in every corner of every playhouse. And Londoners (the living ones) seem to enjoy and celebrate their ghosts more than other people do.

So here is my tour to the most famous, the most notable, the most fascinating—and the most cherished.

THEATRE ROYAL DRURY LANE

Our first stop has got to be the venerable two-hundred-year-old Theatre Royal Drury Lane, which claims to be the world's most haunted theatre. The counterpart of Broadway's Palace for its sheer number of reputed ghosts, and a challenger to both the Belasco and the New Amsterdam for the most vivid and busy ghosts, the Drury Lane is said to host "a veritable ensemble cast of the nether world."

Let's meet a few. But first: parts of this account come from London theatre ghost expert *par excellence* Nick Bromley, who has done a yeoman's job of separating the vast body of legend and conjecture from the truth of actual sightings there, gathered in his book *Stage Ghosts and Haunted Theatres*.

Bromley gives special place to the legend of the Man in Grey at the Drury Lane. (Also known as the "Lane.") As it is told all along Shaftesbury Avenue, the Man in Grey manifests as an eighteenth-century figure of medium height, wearing a long gray cloak, carrying a sword, and sporting a three-cornered hat over a powdered periwig. He's been witnessed by individuals and groups from the 1930s (cast members of *The Dancing Years*) to the 1950s (cast members of *My Fair Lady*) to more recent years. He is known for striding from one side of the upper circle to the other, then exiting with typical supernatural flair directly through a solid wall. The Man in Grey's identity is a matter of debate but it is believed that his visitations, like those of several revenants we've met previously, is an omen of success.

But the Drury Lane displays several other, even more colorful spirits. Joseph Grimaldi (1778–1837) was one of the earliest examples of what we envision as "a clown"—white face with grotesque makeup and wearing colorful clothes. His shows that parodied theatrical conventions of the time evolved into what we now know as British Pantomime. These were not like Marcel Marceau mime shows. They were shows that made fun of a more famous show, as Gerard Alessandrini did with the off-Broadway revue series *Forbidden Broadway*, but with a much bigger budget.

Grimaldi was the top banana in his shows, displaying comedy, Buster Keaton-like violent acrobatics, and his catchphrase, "Here we are again!," which always brought down the house. He was popular for many years at both the Drury Lane and Sadler's Wells. But he gave his body a beating over a lifetime of slaps and tumbles, and died at age fifty-eight.

As he did in life, Grimaldi continues to work both the "Lane" and the "Wells." It's an example of a rare double haunting. He is discovered in both theatres wearing his distinctive clown makeup and wearing white tights (an article of clothing not invented until 1859 by French gymnast Jules Leotard. No, really). For those who find clowns terrifying rather than hilarious, imagine seeing a *clown ghost* appear from behind a door or looking up from your bed. He also sometimes appears as a disembodied clown head. It seems positively Stephen Kingian. But, despite his frightening countenance, Grimaldi doesn't seem to want to hurt or even scare anyone. This is what he wore in life, and back then everybody laughed.

Grimaldi is one of the few ghosts who will actually manifest on a stage in the middle of a performance. One of the Drury Lane ghosts is known to give the occasional young actor a little push to a better part of the stage, or a little pat on the back for a job well done. An invisible Grimaldi is widely assumed to be the prime candidate for this encouraging bit of haunting.

But there are yet other ghosts at the Drury Lane, such as loveable comedian and later-day pantomime comic, the sweet-faced Dan Leno, who plays tricks on the cast and crew. His approach is presaged by the scent of violets. In life he was known to douse himself with violet cologne after a long night of performing.

The Lane also has a royal ghost: King Charles II (1630–1685), who earned the nickname "Merry Monarch" for his partying ways after returning from a long exile. His reign was associated with the raucous theatre movement known as Restoration Comedy that followed more than a decade when theatre was banned in that city. One of the things that made him merriest was his dalliance with his mistress, actress Nell Gwynne, whom he would visit backstage at the Drury Lane. Charles's ghost is said to haunt the theatre, presumably still hoping for one last assignation with Ms. Gwynne.

Interviewed by journalist Andrew Dickinson, actor Nigel Planer, who appeared at the theatre in *Charlie and the Chocolate Factory* in 2013, said he "counts himself a skeptical believer. Interested in the multiplying tales about Drury Lane's star cast of revenants, he took a tour with professional ghost hunter Roger Clarke. Planer was surprised—and, one senses, mildly alarmed—by what he found. 'Everyone in the theatre had some kind of experience. They think they saw the Man in Grey, or they heard a door slam when there was no one in the building. Roger took those stories more seriously than the ghosts: he did think the building had something going on, although it was difficult to say what."

Taken on a tour of the parts of the theatre the public never sees, Dickinson wrote,

> It's in the bowels of the theatre that I get a more realistic sense of why old theatres might inspire so many eerie tales. As we descend through an Escher-like myriad of staircases and along dank, dingy passageways, I am surprised to realize how much I wouldn't want to find myself alone here at night. The "modern" Theatre Royal, built in 1812, is in fact the fourth building to have been raised on this site, which first hosted a theatre

in 1663 (two of its predecessors succumbed to fire, a voracious consumer of theatres in the era of candles and gaslights). Below ground level, we're near the 18th-century foundations: displayed in one corridor are charred beams and what looks, alarmingly, like a human femur, found during restoration. Outside in Covent Garden, the streets are crowded with tourists and lunching office workers; down here, accompanied by the knocking of what I hope is the heating pipes, there's a definite chill in the air.

Planer [his guide] recognizes the sensation. "When you're in here at night after a show, when everyone's left and the only thing on is a little blue light above the stage—I challenge anyone not to be spooked."

THEATRE ROYAL HAYMARKET

Theatre Royal Haymarket, on Suffolk Street facing out on St. James Square, underwent a comprehensive refurbishment in the 1990s. A lot of old memorabilia went into the dumpsters, but one leftover from the old days stayed behind—the ghost of John Baldwin Buckstone (1802–1879) a playwright and comedian who died in 1879 after a long career and a bountiful married life, fathering seventeen children with two wives.

Staff who have seen his ghost say he appears as a short, stout man in a brown suit, not scaring people but radiating good will. He materializes in the Royal box on the opening night of a new play or musical (comedies are his favorite). Such appearances are considered good luck and an omen that the show will be a hit. That said, Buckstone doesn't show himself often, but a 2009 appearance hit the national media. He was seen by actor Ian McKellen during a performance of Samuel Beckett's *Waiting for Godot*. A detailed account of that encounter appears in chapter 6.

Thomas Scott, who hosts the podcast the Bric a Brac Shop said the reason Buckstone haunts the Theatre Royal Haymarket is that "he had a lot of good experiences there." It's part of Scott's theory about what attracts ghost and keeps them locked into a particular place.

> What I find actually is that spirits are always around when there's been an account of energy. Usually it's a bit of a negative energy or bad energy like someone being murdered or some horrible goings-on have happened but it also can work for a positive sense like a lot of good times and happy times and it seems like the spirit will be there as well. So, it seems like the spirits come around for the energies. . . . There are theories that we're actually watching a replay of emotions that have taken place in that particular time in space. I believe that quantum physics will actually have an answer to all of these things.
>
> But if you look through all the sightings of spirits and ghosts, it's always when there's been a heightening of emotion good times or bad times. It seems . . . John Baldwin Buckstone enjoyed being at the Theatre Royal. He had a very good time there and he comes back to it. It's almost a bit like tradition for the actors today because they know if someone sees his spirit it means their show is going to be a hit. It usually appears for

comedies and a successful show, which is what his theatre was known for when he managed it. It was one of the top theatres to go and see a comedy act. . . . John Baldwin Buckstone is one of the happy spirits and quite a good omen to be seen if you actually see him.

The Haymarket is believed to host another former manager as a ghost: David Edward Morris, whose spirit returns to the theatre, *Brigadoon*-like for one night, roughly once a decade.

COLISEUM THEATRE

I'll ask you to remove your hats for the next London ghost—a young man who gave his all for his country. The Coliseum Theatre in St. Martin's Lane, is haunted by several spirits, including a World War I soldier who takes a seat in the second row. The soldier was relieved to be on leave from the meat grinder of the battlefront against the Germans. On the last day of his leave, he took in a show at the Coliseum. The color, beauty, and music of the show may have been his last happy memory on this earth, because shortly after returning to battle, he was killed in action.

He was first glimpsed and recognized when a group of his army buddies, on a similar leave near the end of "The Great War," spotted him walking down the aisle toward them—and then vanishing. Word of the story got out, and people reported seeing the lost soldier walking in, and even sitting in, the Coliseum for more than a decade.

GARRICK THEATRE

The Garrick Theatre at 2 Charing Cross Road was built in 1835. The theatre enjoyed one of its greatest periods of success around the turn of the twentieth century when it was managed by Arthur Bourchier, who also starred in many of his own productions of the classics. Like the American manager (and Bourchier's contemporary) David Belasco, he lived in an apartment above the theatre, and had a special staircase built so he could oversee his productions whenever he wished.

He left the theatre and attempted a career in politics before his death in 1927. Those convenient steps he built are now famous as the West End's "Phantom Staircase." Bourchier is sometimes seen descending the staircase, and is said to offer actors "an encouraging (if unsettling) pat on the back," à la Grimaldi, the Drury Lane clown.

PRINCE EDWARD THEATRE

Laura Schoenfelder, director of operations at Audience Rewards in New York, learned of several ghosts while working as merchandise manager for *Mary Poppins* at the Prince Edward Theatre in the West End. These included the Pink Lady and the Smoking Man, a.k.a. Cigar Man. "The Pink Lady is a dancer who died falling off the Grand Tier of the auditorium in, I think, the 1940s. Stories about her say she's a playful ghost and likes to mess with people. Some people I know have seen her and thought she was a patron, but then she would disappear after they told her the house was closed. One colleague said she heard her making noise so called out that she was glad she was having fun, but would she mind stopping until my colleague left—and she did! The house management would get emails from patrons saying they felt someone breathing on the back of their necks during the show."

Schoenfelder said, "I'm not sure who the Smoking Man was in life, just that his ghost had the reputation of being mean. After performances, one of the VIP rooms in the stalls would always start to smell of cigar smoke. I had to walk through that room to get to the merch stand at the end of each night when most of the lights were out and I always smelled the smoke. I'd often call out that I was just walking through and wouldn't be there long, so he knew I wasn't there to disturb him."

ADELPHI THEATRE

The Adelphi Theatre on the Strand is haunted by the ghost of William Terriss, an actor who was straight-up murdered at the theatre's stage door in 1897.

The debonair Terriss (nicknamed "Breezy Bill"), who specialized in athletic, handsome-hero roles like Mercutio and Robin Hood, was starring in the melodrama *Secret Service* as a Union spy during the American Civil War who falls in love with a Southern lady.

Terriss knew his killer well. Richard Archer Prince was a fellow actor, down on his luck, whom Terriss had helped professionally and financially for years. But Prince had trouble finding and keeping jobs because of his alcoholism, which rendered him increasingly unstable mentally. Despite Terriss's generosity, Prince got it into his head that Terriss had insulted him, and the two had a violent argument a few days before the murder. When a subsequent request for money was refused, Prince lay in wait, knowing that Terriss usually accessed the theatre via the Royal entrance on Maiden Lane. When Terriss arrived for the evening's performance on December 16, 1897, Prince leaped out of his hiding place and stabbed his benefactor to death.

Terriss's shade is known to appear, not only inside the Adelphi, but in the nearby Covent Garden Underground station. The murder is memorialized by a plaque at the theatre, near the spot where Breezy Bill's life was taken in a manner that would have handsomely befitted one of the melodramas that were his specialty.

HER MAJESTY'S THEATRE

The majestically named Herbert Beerbohm Tree (1852–1917) oversaw the 1897–1899 rebuilding of the 1705-vintage Her Majesty's Theatre on Haymarket. He then became its manager for the rest of his life, mounting spectacular revivals of Shakespeare plays, but also presenting premieres of new works by George Bernard Shaw and others. Tree was a towering presence in the world of London theatre, with numerous credits, including the founding of the training program now known as the Royal Academy of Dramatic Arts (RADA).

Like other actor-managers of his time, he lived "over the store" in an apartment above the theatre. No impediment as minor as mere death would keep him from continuing his supervision of "his" theatre. However, unlike the ghost of clown Joseph Grimaldi, who finds time in the afterlife to haunt two theatres, Tree's ghost is very particular about the location of his haunting. He appears only in the house-left top box. Sometimes he's visible as a transparent figure; sometimes the door to the box swings open by itself; sometimes he manifests only as one of the dreadful icy spots that seems popular with so many of our phantoms.

The last word is used deliberately, as the theatre has been home to Andrew Lloyd Webber's *The Phantom of the Opera* since it opened there in 1986.

THE OLD VIC

The theatre now known as the Old Vic dates from 1818, one of the few current theatres operating in the Southwark section of London on the south bank of the Thames River—not far from the site of Shakespeare's original Globe Theatre.

Over its two centuries of existence, the venerable old playhouse with its distinctive white façade, has accumulated several spooks, phantoms, and poltergeists, but the mother spirit of the playhouse is its former manager, Lilian Baylis (1874–1937). She was responsible for running both the Old Vic near the south end of London and Sadler's Wells near the north end. She also ran an opera company, so she was forever on the move.

Perhaps worn out by her stresses and peregrinations, she died of a heart attack at age sixty-three, on the eve of the opening of Shakespeare's "cursed" play *Macbeth*, starring Judith Anderson and Laurence Olivier. She manifests at the Old Vic by the sound of a disembodied violin playing long after the audience has departed. She sometimes materializes in full figure, which is how she was identified by those who knew her.

In keeping with a good manager's ability to delegate responsibility, Baylis even has a partner ghost, an unknown actress who accompanies her and dramatically displays blood-drenched hands, à la Lady Macbeth.

But there are more ghosts, some who predate Baylis's tenure. Before the theatre was reconfigured, its expansive balcony seated more than one thousand, accessed by narrow stairways. Those staircases became the scene of several deaths caused by crowd surges trying to press through, up or down. These deaths came to be known as "The Boxing Day Curse," because they all occurred on the day after Christmas, a U.K. holiday, traditionally used for shopping and going out—especially to the theatre. In 1858, the toll was sixteen deaths from people trying to flee a small fire that had broken out on the stage. Several of the victims are reported to haunt the balcony, which has been substantially reduced in size.

PALACE THEATRE

The imposing red-brick Palace Theatre sits on Shaftesbury Avenue like the Queen of Theatreland. Many great hits have played there, most recently the two-part *Harry Potter and the Cursed Child.*

The witches and wizards of Hogwarts aren't the only supernatural characters to be found there. The theatre is traditionally said to be haunted by two ghosts. One is the great British theatre composer Ivor Novello (1893–1951), a contemporary of "Golden Age" American songwriters Cole Porter, Richard Rodgers, and the rest of their generation. Novello was enormously popular in Great Britain but failed to find comparable success in the United States. Novello is said to be seen watching shows from the Dress Circle. For many years, the managers of the Palace kept two seats bolted open so Novello and his unseen guest would always have a comfortable place to survey the stage.

Among those he might be watching: the ghost of Russian-born prima ballerina Anna Pavlova (1881–1931), who adopted England as her home in 1912 and died of pleurisy in 1931 after refusing an operation to save her life because she was told she would never be able to dance again afterward. At the Palace, her spirit is sometimes seen going through her steps on the stage.

BROOKSIDE THEATRE

Though haunted theatres abound across Great Britain, I've focused mainly on some notable London ghosts. However, I'd like to add one more from outside the West End: the Brookside Theatre in Romford, Essex. Public interest in theatre ghosts was piqued in 2014 when a security camera at the Brookside captured a disturbing sight: chairs inside this tiny theatre sliding around as if being pushed by . . . something . . . a few hours after psychic medium Roy Roberts held a show there. The forty-four-second clip isn't very dramatic, but no one has come forward with a reasonable explanation of what caused it.

11

OTHER INTERNATIONAL GHOSTS

Ghosts have been reported in all places and in all times. In the first century CE, Roman author Pliny the Younger reported the story of a philosopher named Athenodorus who bought a house said to be haunted. It wasn't long before the ghost appeared to Athenodorus. The ghost was bound in chains but was able to lead his new landlord to the place where he had been murdered and where his body was buried. The cool, calm Athenodorus marked the location, then dug on the spot and found a skeleton bound similarly in chains. After the correct burial rites, the bones were reinterred with honor, after which the ghost walked no more.

The same is true today. There are hundreds of reports of haunted theatres in nearly all countries. But I've picked out a few of the most dramatic, most heartbreaking, and most hair-raising.

PALAIS GARNIER, PARIS

When people hear that there is a theatre ghost in Paris, they say, well, of course! The Phantom of the Opera! Gastón Leroux's 1910 novel about a mysterious, half-mad masked musical genius who falls in love with a young soprano, kidnaps her, and takes her to his lair deep below the opera house is the source material for the long-running Andrew Lloyd Webber musical. The novel and its many adaptations, including the iconic 1925 Lon Chaney silent film, draw on incidents from the actual history of the Paris Opéra's Palais Garnier, which opened in 1875. A counterweight for an ornate seven-ton grand chandelier did indeed fall through ceiling there and kill a concierge. The basement is indeed honeycombed with passageways that lead down to a lake-like underground water storage tank. There was also once a severely burned and disfigured hermit named Erik (also sometimes called Ernest) who once sheltered in the tunnels and doubtless inspired Leroux, who claimed that there really was a Phantom.

Today, the magnificent Second Empire edifice's management encourages ghost lovers. Private booth five, which the fictional Phantom demands be kept available exclusively for him, is actually marked with a brass plaque that reads "Loge de Fantôme de l'Opéra."

But it should be remembered that even in the fictionalized book and musical, the Phantom was not depicted as an actual ghost, but as an extremely troubled (living) man who presented himself as "O.G.": Opera Ghost. Which is not to say that ghosts don't haunt its catacombs, catwalks, and dressing rooms.

The true phantom of the Palais Garnier is not a man at all but an older woman, reportedly rejected by the man she loved, who wanders the building and sometimes appears in the surrounding streets and alleyways, reportedly searching for her lost sweetheart.

EDINBURGH PLAYHOUSE, EDINBURGH, SCOTLAND

Edinburgh boasts a host of haunted places, including a churchyard, an old dungeon, a museum, an alleyway, and many more paranormal spots. But none seem so thoroughly drenched in ectoplasm as the Edinburgh Playhouse at 18-22 Greenside Place in the Scottish capital.

The theatre was built in the late 1920s on the site of earlier theatres dating back to the fourteenth century. It houses several wraiths, but none as active as Albert, the original stage doorman of the Playhouse who "died alone at the building late one winter's night," according to the *Edinburgh News*.

His first recorded sighting occurred under strange circumstances in the 1950s. There are several stories about this encounter but all involve local police called to investigate a supposed nighttime break-in. Arriving at the theatre and finding the stage door unlocked and ajar, the constable commenced a search of the building to find the intruder. Upstairs, the officer found an old man who identified himself as Albert the doorman and said there had been no break-in after all. Mollified by the doorman's promises to lock up and be more careful, the officer left.

The policeman checked in at the theatre the next day and told the daytime doorman that there had been no problem, just the nighttime doorman doing his rounds. "The ashen-faced stage door man explained to him that Albert had died some time previously," and there had been no one at the theatre that night."

Some ghosts go out of their way to appear and disappear peacefully. Albert isn't one of them. He manifests as a cold, dark, formed mist. When it passes in front of light, the light dims, then brightens again as it passes. Keith Donald, the theatre's more recent doorman, was quoted by the *News* saying that in his first encounter, he was doing his nightly rounds accompanied by his dog, Meg. Meg suddenly seemed unwilling to enter one of the theatre's familiar towers. "So I put her lead [leash] on her and tried to get her to come with me but she literally went rigid, looked at me, then to the top of the stairs, and then back at me as she started moaning and whining. That was enough for me, the South Tower didn't get checked that night."

Donald ran into Albert again, and in the process suffered what he called "the most frightening experience" of his life. "There are two sets of doors from the foyer to the auditorium and there is a light between them," he explained. "As I approached the first set of doors I realized it was dark between them. I went to investigate but as I got closer, the light suddenly came on. Chills began to run down my spine as I realized that the darkness which had blocked the light had moved into the auditorium. The closer I got to it, the further it receded. Terrified by this time I was determined to find out what it was so forced myself to go into the auditorium. . . . The stage right box was lit as normal, but the stage left box was shrouded, at about five per cent of its usual output and I got the awful feeling that something didn't want me to be there."

There was another dog-related encounter in 1997. As the chosen site of a Commonwealth Heads of Government meeting, the Playhouse was searched by a team of bomb-sniffing police dogs. When they got to the theatre's Level Six, however, the dogs refused to enter. Nothing would induce them to get close to it.

In the end Donald had to call in a dog team from the military. They went in and cleared the floor without a problem. So here's the kicker: Donald recalls, "Jokingly, I asked if this was because army dogs were 'harder' than police jobs. . . . 'No,' came the reply 'but they're based at the Castle so they are used to spooks and spirits.' Put in that matter of fact way, it was quite chilling."

Perhaps the dogs were spooked by Albert. Or, perhaps it was the ghost of the Great Lafayette (née Sigmund Neuberger), a popular illusionist who died on the stage of the theatre when a burning lamp fell over and caused a fire that killed him and ten others. The Great Lafayette manifests by shining his sparkling rings at visitors in dark rooms.

LA SCALA OPERA HOUSE, MILAN, ITALY

Milan, the arts capital of Italy, is full of uber-creepy haunted spots, including the church of San Bernardino alle Ossa, which is "decorated" with the skulls and other bones of plague victims and criminals who suffered the death penalty. But the city's cultural centerpiece, La Scala opera house, is said to be haunted by the spirit of volcanic *diva assoluta* Maria Callas (1927–1977), who startles visitors with appearances, reportedly as revenge for once being booed during a performance there. *Callas in Concert*, a performance featuring a ghostly 3D hologram of La Divina lip-synching to recordings of her triumphs, toured in 2018.

BOWMAN ARTS CENTER, LETHBRIDGE, CANADA

Among the many notable Canadian theatre ghosts are the spirits of two women who died under wrenching circumstances.

A young Chinese-Canadian woman was beaten to death in the women's restroom at the Bowman Arts Center in Lethbridge, Alberta. What set off her attackers? The other women in the restroom had mistaken her for a boy, as she was wearing a traditional Chinese-style outfit. Her sobs and cries of pain reportedly can still be heard there.

The other is a bride of the 1920s who was jilted by her intended husband a few days before their wedding. In despair, she hanged herself in a room she was renting on an upper floor of the Princess Theatre building in Edmonton, Alberta. In a grand white dress she can sometimes be seen descending the theatre's grand staircase. She looks like a ghostly princess at the Princess Theatre, and that is the name by which she is known.

PRINCESS THEATRE, MELBOURNE, AUSTRALIA

On the other side of the world is another haunted Princess Theatre. The Princess is not just the oldest theatre in Melbourne, Australia, it's also reputed to be the most haunted in the country. And that's all thanks to Fred Baker, a bass-baritone who left his homeland in Italy, changed his name to the much more operatic Frederick Federici, and made a new life for himself in 1880s Melbourne.

Jesse Cain from the Princess said that Fred was appearing in the role of the devil's familiar Mephistopheles in a spectacular production of Gounod's *Faust* at the theatre, when he joined the ranks of the supernatural. The opera tells the story of a Dr. Faustus who offers to sell his soul to the devil (Mephistopheles) in return for knowledge, but then tries to change his mind. Federici's death happened suddenly the evening of March 3, 1888, as he was returning in triumph to Hell with Dr. Faustus's soul (actually being lowered through a trap door into the trap below the stage), he suffered a massive heart attack and passed on to his own posthumous reward.

Before the demanding performance that evening, he reportedly said, "I will give a fine performance tonight, but it will kill me."

That's apocryphal. But here's the strange part: it seems that after finishing the performance, he didn't want to be robbed of his hard-earned curtain call. As the theatre employees were trying to revive him in the basement, others in the cast claim that he came out on stage as usual and took his well-earned bows by their side.

Federici went out the way many actors say they'd like to go: in the middle of a star performance, in a great costume, to the applause of devoted fans.

And well over a century later Federici still appears regularly at the theatre, attired in period evening dress. He also sometimes appears in dressing rooms, as if he's getting ready to go on again. His materialization on opening nights is said to be a token of a hit. For many years, a third-row seat in the Princess Theatre Dress Circle was left empty at each performance for his use.

Cain said, "Fred is very much a benevolent presence, nothing nasty ever happens. He's more of a friendly poltergeist."

THEATRO MUNICIPAL, SÃO PAULO, BRAZIL

Brazilians are a proud people, forever striving to get the respect they deserve on the world stage. In 1911 the city fathers of São Paulo, the country's largest city, spent millions on a sumptuous temple of culture called the Theatro Municipal (Municipal Theatre) designed to attract classical music, ballet, jazz, and opera stars from Europe, the United States, and elsewhere around the world. More than twenty thousand people reportedly attended its opening performances. This showcase was also credited with helping to inspire and launch the native Brazilian Modernist Movement, which influenced culture in the South American country for the rest of the twentieth century and beyond.

So much creative energy was focused on this single edifice that the spirits of these native artists appear to have stuck to the building permanently. Employees working there at night report pianos starting to play by themselves, the echoing sound of operatic voices echoing in the empty performing spaces, and costumed figures moving in the vacant dressing rooms long after the artists who used them had left for the day. Another happy ghost story—the next one, not so much.

MANILA FILM CENTER, MANILA, THE PHILIPPINES

The Manila Film Center in the capital of the Philippines offers an especially macabre lesson on the price of greed. The cinema was planned as a centerpiece of the brand-new $25 million Cultural Center of the Philippines, as envisioned by Imelda Marcos, wife of the country's dictator Ferdinand Marcos. The complex was scheduled to open in January 1982 with a grand inaugural Manila Film Festival at the Film Center, which was designed to resemble the Parthenon in Athens. The films were booked, tickets were sold, but the actual construction of the theatre fell behind schedule. With the country's (and its leaders') prestige (and ego) on the line, intense pressure was exerted on project supervisor Betty Benitez. Some four thousand workers labored in three shifts around the clock. This led to rushed work and the inevitable cutting of corners—with fatal effect.

At 3 a.m. on November 17, 1981 while frenzied workers slaved against the impossible deadline, the scaffolding supporting the fourth floor collapsed, sending some two hundred workers plunging to the first floor. Some were impaled on steel rebar. Others, believed to number one hundred sixty-nine people, plunged into freshly poured fast-drying concrete and were buried alive.

Learning how much time it would take to recover the bodies, Marcos ordered that they be left in the concrete and the job completed. Accurate figures were hard to ascertain, since all media coverage was banned. Supernatural activities reportedly began almost immediately, with surviving workers reporting that they saw their supposedly dead comrades showing up for work, and happily believing they had survived after all—and then they vanished.

Despite the ghastly disaster, Marcos got her way. The Manila Film Center bowed on schedule January 18, 1982, drawing international stars to the opening feature, *Gandhi*. But the ghosts of the dead were having none of it. Attendees, who didn't realize they were sitting above a mass grave, reported feeling a creepy icy presence in different parts of the theatre, and usherettes complained of a strange odor backstage. The festival and its halfhearted sequel in 1983 were such financials flops that the theatre was abandoned for years.

HUGUANG OPERA HOUSE IN BEIJING, CHINA

Among the oldest still-operating theatres in the world is the 1807-vintage Huguang Huiguan Opera House in Beijing, which has survived more than two hundred years of political upheaval in that country. But, of course, ghosts don't usually care about earthly politics.

This friendly-looking, red-painted theatre and museum was built with the best of intentions, but we know where that intentions-paved road often leads. Once home to the Beijing Opera, the theatre abuts the site of an ancient cemetery. A well-meaning philanthropist built housing for the city's homeless over the cemetery, and the interred weren't very happy about it.

Their spirits were held at bay by a janitor who was disfigured by leprosy. The sight of him intimidated even the dead. Since his death, however, those who work at the theatre report that the adjoining courtyard is haunted by spirits who can be heard shrieking there. A special feature: if visiting audience members toss a stone onto the grounds of the courtyard, a disembodied voice can sometimes be heard scolding the miscreant.

ST. JAMES THEATRE, WELLINGTON, NEW ZEALAND

Most of these ghost stories come from the Northern Hemisphere, but New Zealand boasts one of the most colorfully haunted theatres south of the Tropic of Capricorn.

The stately St. James Theatre in the capital city of Wellington was built in 1912 as a vaudeville house. Its fortunes rose and fell with the times and was nearly given up and demolished. But the Wellington business and theatre communities rose up in the late 1980s and raised $18.5 million for a full-scale restoration with the help of Sam Wanamaker, the same benefactor who helped rebuild Shakespeare's Globe Theatre in London.

All the hubbub, though, doesn't seem to have ruffled the theatre's several colorful ghosts. The star of the supernatural bill is Yuri, a Russian ballet dancer who stumbled (or, as some believe, was pushed) and fell fifty feet from a catwalk in the fly space and died when he hit the stage.

St. James historian David McGill has interviewed many employees who had encounters with Yuri and believe in his existence implicitly. Yuri is not only one of the busiest theatre ghosts, he's also one of the most benevolent—even lifesaving.

Jim Hutchinson was nine years a projectionist at the Saint James and believes Yuri saved him and his family's life on separate occasions in the 1960s. "I was dressing the stage late one night. About midnight I was up on the fly floor and about to head back down when the lights went out. I knew the area pretty well and thought I was by the safety rail, beside the ladder. I felt this very strong feeling of being pushed backwards, and this intense cold, like I had a packet of frozen peas on my chest. I looked closely where I was about to step. There was a drop of ten meters. I was several meters from where I thought I was."

The second time he was working down stage, his wife and eight-month-old son were upstage. "She was mending the gold curtains," he said. "I heard a funny noise and a beam [of wood] was coming down. I was pushed backwards. So was my wife. Our son was floating backwards to the wall, about three meters. The beam would have hit where we were standing. It hadn't been tied properly and there were no counterweights." . . . Hutchinson thanks Yuri for saving his family's lives.

Jim Ahern was projectionist there in 1977 when he encountered Yuri. "I was pulling aside the masking for the Cinemascope screen. It was freezing though it was a hot day. I had heard the stories about Yuri. I saw this tall, thin man in a black suit, aged about 30. He was walking straight toward me. I said 'Hello Yuri.' He vanished. I didn't tell anybody at first in case they thought I had gone mad."

Ahern agreed to take part in a séance to contact the theatre's ghosts.

The ouija board spelled out Yuri's story of a woman called Pasha pushing him from the flies to his death. Jim says he did not feel frightened by this, but felt safe with Yuri about.

John Blake was theatre manager from 1972 to 1977. Like Bob after him, he spent his working day from 11 AM walking around the darkened theatre with a [flashlight], until he switched on the lights for the 5 PM session. In the dark, Yuri was always alongside. "When I started here," Blake said, "I heard the ghost stories and I admit I was scared. I used to tell myself they were just rubbish. But after a while I got used to Yuri and his habits—like tugging curtains back, throwing a row of seats down, pulling light bulbs out. One trick of his was to [wait] till I'd turned all the house lights out at night and I was over the road getting into my car, then turn all the lights on again. The whole place would blaze, and of course I'd have to go back and turn everything off again. That was his sense of humor."

Blake saw him just once. I was walking through the green door on my way to pull back the heavy iron door that separates the stage from the rest of the theatre. And there he was, like a mist. I was so scared I automatically turned and headed for the main doors leading to the street dash and there was a fire brigade outside, apparently come in answer to a false alarm. Whether Yuri was warning me there was a possible fire, or just that the brigade was on its way, I'll never know."

Apparently Yuri is not alone in the shadows of the St. James. The theatre is also haunted by a spirit known only as the Wailing Woman, because she can be heard sobbing and keening around the deserted theatre. She often presents as a woman with a screaming face, and sometimes the screaming face is a sickening green color. According to legend, this aspiring actress tried to stage a career comeback at the theatre in the 1940s, but was booed off the stage. In despair she fled to one of the small dressing rooms off the mezzanine and committed suicide by slitting her wrists.

The Wailing Woman is not as friendly as Yuri. In fact, she has been blamed for sabotaging the performances of other female performers. One fell from a ladder and another sprained an ankle just before going on. Yet another was about to sing a featured opera role when she unaccountably lost her voice.

The St. James is also said to be haunted by an entire ghostly boys' choir.

Another time Hutchinson heard a boys choir in the empty stage area. He went looking for the radio. There was none. The

187

sound shifted to the other side of the stage. He went to that side. The sound shifted back. He thought it strange, then forgot about it, until he heard of the boys choir that had played the St. James at the beginning of the war, sailed off, and they and their ship were never seen again.

12

GHOSTS OF THE PAST

Ⅰf the Broadway of today is haunted by ghosts, so much more so was the Broadway of the pre–World War II era, when there was double the number of theatres. Many of these ghosts disappeared when their theatres were torn down in the holocaust of theatres in the 1950s and 1960s. But their creepy stories, passed down by theatre old-timers, live on.

METROPOLITAN OPERA HOUSE

Since the 1960s the Metropolitan Opera of New York has reposed in architect Wallace Harrison's travertine temple that serves as the center-piece of Lincoln Center for the Performing Arts. But it was not always headquartered there.

For many years, the opera house stood at the corner of 39th Street and Broadway, anchoring the stretch of Broadway between Herald Square and Times Square known then as the Rialto. The greatest opera stars of the early and mid-twentieth century held forth there from 1883 to the mid-1960s, when the building was demolished and replaced with an office tower. (A bank on the main floor has opera scenes painted on the walls of its downstairs office, but a query of some of the tellers there revealed that only one had any idea of why.)

One of the attractions of the old Met was Frances Alda, a.k.a. Madame Frances, a haughty diva who became an unusually attention-seeking ghost following her death. Her spirit would appear amid the audience during performances.

Barbara Smith, in her book *Haunted Theaters*, recorded a typical Madame Frances materialization:

> The best documented visitation by Alda's ghost occurred early in the opera season in 1955. A woman whose companion was unexpectedly unable to accompany her turned the spare ticket in at the box office. By intermission that solo patron had become extremely irate and sought out the head usher. It seemed that the person who bought the ticket for the seat next to her disregarded every rule of audience etiquette.
>
> The angry woman described a ring-laden dowager who voiced disparaging comments every time the evening's female lead began to sing. Worse, she would punctuate her every comment with an elbow to the patron's ribs. Even when other performers took the stage, this incredibly rude person would fidget with her program, thereby causing further disturbance.
>
> Understandably, the woman, who was already disappointed not to be attending the opera with her friend, wanted the administration of the hall to do something about this intolerable distraction. Those in authority were willing to do so, but their actions were certainly not what the patron had

expected they would be. Rather than warning the nuisance that her behavior would no longer be permitted, a director of the house took the complainant aside. After giving her a glass of sherry, the employee explained to the woman that she would be able to enjoy the rest of the opera in peace. He knew this fact because the perpetrator was well known to the staff at the Met. She was the ghost of the long deceased prima donna Frances Alda, who had never been known to stay past the first act.

Madame Frances appears to have moved on to the next world when the building was torn down in 1967. There is no record of her appearing at the bank.

EMPIRE THEATRE

Broadway's New Amsterdam Theatre is known as the "House Beautiful" for its nature-based art nouveau trimmings. But once upon a time it had a rival, just a few blocks downtown and east—the magnificently elegant Empire Theatre. It was built in 1893 at 40th Street and Broadway by Charles Frohman, another of the producer-managers in the mold of David Belasco. During a career that lasted from 1889 to 1915, Frohman produced an astonishing 339 shows on Broadway alone (plus many more around the United States), most of them utterly forgotten wisps, but some that were solid hits, such as *Sherlock Holmes*, *Secret Service*, and *The Girl from Utah*; some Shakespearean classics with big period stars; some that have important places in theatre history like Edmond Rostand's *L'Aiglon* and *Les Romanesques* (the latter play the basis for the musical *The Fantasticks*); plus a few enduring classics, like the first American production of Oscar Wilde's *The Importance of Being Earnest*. Frohman was also a special champion of prolific playwright Clyde Fitch, later purported to have become a ghost himself.

However, Frohman's enduring legacy to theatre, world culture, and the imaginations of countless children was a play about a boy who wouldn't grow up, *Peter Pan* by Scotsman J. M. Barrie, starring Maude Adams. Peter first flew to Neverland at the Empire Theatre on November 6, 1905, as Frohman and Barrie nodded happily in the wings.

In addition to serving as Barrie's producer, Frohman became his friend and consultant. A decade later, in 1915, Barrie was struggling with his new show in London with an opulent title, *Rosy Rapture, the Pride of the Beauty Chorus*. Barrie implored Frohman to come over and take a look. In this era before transatlantic commercial air transport, the wealthy Frohman booked passage on a luxury liner headed for England, the RMS *Lusitania*. World War I was already raging in Europe with Great Britain and the German Empire as enemy combatants. The German embassy had openly warned travelers about the danger of being afloat in ships flying the British flag.

Enter Frohman's theatre superintendent, John Ryland, a rare African American boss at a time when segregation was accepted policy in most areas of American life. Frohman was ahead of his time in his advocacy for diversity in the workplace. He told Ryland that he wasn't concerned about the threat. The *Lusitania* was a passenger ship, not a warship. Ryland took Frohman to the dock on May 1 and helped him get his luggage loaded onto the mighty craft. They shook hands and Ryland watched the *Lusitania* disappear over the horizon. It was scheduled to arrive in England May 7.

On May 6, when Frohman was supposed to be nearly across the Atlantic, Ryland was closing up Frohman's producing offices on the fifth floor of the Empire building when he stopped still. There he saw his employer, sitting at his desk as usual, with papers and photographs spread out before him. When Ryland said, "I thought you were almost in Europe by this time." Frohman reportedly replied, "No, John, I had to come back. I had to look at all this again before I left. Leave me alone here for a few minutes. Thanks."

Ryland contacted several other employees to tell them what he had witnessed. They didn't believe him and returned to the theatre, trouping upstairs to Frohman's office to see what he had seen. When they arrived, the lights were out and the office was again in its normal order. Ryland got ribbed pretty badly for his little "joke."

The next morning they were astonished at the banner headlines on every newspaper. The *Lusitania* had been sunk by a German submarine. According to later counts, of the 1,962 people on board, 1,198 died. Frohman was listed as "missing" at first, but his body later washed up on the shore of Ireland. According to one account, as the ship was sinking, Frohman quoted *Peter Pan*, saying, "Why fear death? It is the most beautiful adventure that life gives one."

Frohman's production company, Charles Frohman Inc., continued in other hands until the late 1930s.

In 1953, the Empire was ripped down to make way for a faceless office building. Down it came, as old-time employees wept on the sidewalk across the street. What did Frohman's ghost think? Did he move on? Did he visit the Lunt-Fontanne Theatre in 2015 to see himself portrayed by Kelsey Grammer in the musical *Finding Neverland*? Did he just go home (see his entry in chapter 5). Or is he spending eternity wandering the unfamiliar glass and steel offices where the Empire once stood, wondering what happened to his Broadway?

LYRIC THEATRE

As mentioned previously, Clyde Fitch was one of the most prolific and successful playwrights of the late nineteenth and early twentieth centuries, and was even said to have had a brief affair with English playwright Oscar Wilde. His *Beau Brummel*, *Captain Jinks of the Horse Marines*, and *Barbara Frietchie* enjoyed long runs for their time and were repeatedly revived. Fitch knew how to make an entrance—and an exit. He died in September 1909 in Europe at age forty-four of appendicitis while his last play, *The City*, was in rehearsal.

On opening night, December 21, 1909, at the Lyric on 42nd Street, after the supporting players and the stars took their bows at the final curtain, the audience filled with his friends and fans was aghast to see Fitch himself appear from the wings, come to center stage, bow, and vanish. Now that's a special effect!

MUSIC PALACE THEATRE

There was a time when the Music Palace theatre at the corner of Bowery and Hester Streets in New York's Chinatown was a family-run neighborhood center, showing Chinese-language films, mostly from Hong Kong and Taiwan.

But over the years a malevolent cluster of ghosts so thoroughly took over the building that patrons started avoiding it. Ghosts included a Peeping Tom spirit who haunted the ladies' room and drew complaints from the moviegoers. There was also a mischievous ghost who would grab people's legs from under their seats. When victims spun around, there was no one there. The cinema finally closed, and the building remained boarded up for more than a decade because no one would buy it. It was finally demolished and is now the site of the Windham Garden Hotel.

WALLACK'S THEATRE

New York had two theatres named Wallack's at different times, both named for the theatre producing family of James W. Wallack (known as "the Governor") and his son, Lester Wallack. The first theatre that bore their name stood on Broadway at 13th Street, and was known as the Star Theatre for many years. It was torn down in 1901. The second Wallack's Theatre rose on Broadway at the corner of 30th Street in 1881, and had its last performance in 1915.

The closing and imminent demolition of the second Wallack's Theatre inspired the *New York Times* to print an unusual story, "The Ghost Haunt Goes When Wallacks' Goes," which includes this anecdote from the first Wallack's:

> When he first came to America James W. Wallach was thrown from a stage[coach] going from New Brunswick to Philadelphia and his leg was broken. After that, he always walked with a cane. He had been buried three weeks when the night watchman in the 13th Street playhouse on his rounds through the building heard the footsteps of the Governor, punctuated by the heavier thump of his cane.

"I heard the steps crossing the stage," the night watchman used to say. "As I walked down the side aisle toward the stage, they came, step, step, thump; step, step, thump. Just as I had heard them on many a night after the audience had gone and the Governor was leaving the theatre. For the instant I forgot I had seen him in his coffin a little while before, and as they drew nearer I stepped aside in the hallway behind the boxes to let him pass, just as I had done scores of times. 'Goodnight, Governor,' I said, and he thumped, thumped past and on down the aisle just as natural as life. It was not till the sound had died away that I realized the Governor was dead and in his grave, and when I stopped running I was in Union Square."

One night more than thirty years later [manager] Mr. Burnham was working in the box office of the Star Theater, when he noticed a boy standing talking to the house fireman in the lobby. The fireman, who had been on duty in the theatre for years and was a quiet man who did his duty thoroughly and said little, was as pale as death, and Mr. Burnham, noticing this, called the boy and asked what the matter was.

"Tom says he's seen a ghost," said the boy. Mr. Burnham called to the fireman, who crossed the lobby and spoke with difficulty. "Mr. Burnham," he said, "I don't think I'm a coward; I've faced death in the flames many times and would cheerfully do so again; but I wouldn't go downstairs again if my job depended on it. I have just seen the ghost of Wallack down there. . . . I was close to him as I am standing to you, and he looked as real as you. No, Sir; I'll never go down there again."

Mr. Burnham was deeply interested in this report of a . . . spectral visitor. He had known the fireman for a long time as a brave, unimpressionable man, and the real terror under which he was laboring when he told his story was patent. So he went on a tour of investigation. The basement was formerly fitted up as a bar, a refreshment room as they used to call it, but now it had become a storeroom. At the foot of the stairs he found a pile of furniture covered with white dust cloths, and a few feet away stood a three-sheet [full size] poster of Mr. [James] Haworth in the [title] role in *Rosedale* in which Wallack played many times. Mr. Burnham reached the conclusion that the fireman, who knew the actor well and had seen [him] hundreds of times on the stage and about the theatre, through some psychic association of the sight of Haworth's picture in Wallack's familiar role, the ghostly dust cloths . . . of having met Wallack in perhaps the identical spot, received the illusion which so startled him.

Strangely enough, when the old Star was torn down, behind a blind wall in the basement near the spot where the firemen had met Wallack's ghost, was found a portrait of the actor. It was dusty and moldy with age, and had probably stood against the wall when the workmen came to brick in the false wall, and, unnoticed by them in the darkness, had been entombed.

EASTSIDE PLAYHOUSE

We've seen that some ghosts are indeed friendly, but there are few to match Herkimer, the operetta-loving ghost last seen at the now-defunct

Eastside Playhouse, 334 East 74th Street in New York City. That was the longtime headquarters of LOOM (the Light Opera of Manhattan), and Herkimer didn't haunt the theatre building itself; he haunted LOOM. *Playbill* reported, "He has been with that company from the beginning at their first location, St. Michael's Church, and moved with them to the Jan Hus [Playhouse] and then to their current location. His favorite show is *The Pirates of Penzance* and he has been known to move props about if they are not in the right place. He mostly stays in the theatre's balcony, but occasionally he has been seen onstage, tap dancing and humming. He's a happy musical ghost."

PRINCESS THEATRE, MONTREAL

Master illusionist and escape artist Harry Houdini (1874–1926) was discussed at length in chapter 2, along with many places he is alleged to be haunting.

But one of them deserves a slightly closer look, partly because it is the place that he received the injury that would kill him, and partly because it weathered a large number of Houdini appearances—but is now gone: the old Princess Theatre at 476 Rue Sainte-Catherine Oest, Montreal, Quebec.

Houdini traveled North America in vaudeville, performing his amazing feats of "magic" and endurance. One of his "bits" was challenging members of the audience to punch him in the stomach as hard as they could, with no adverse effect. Because Houdini kept himself, including his core, in top condition, he was able to tense his abdominal muscles in a way that protected him from injury.

On this day in October 1926, Houdini was in his dressing room at the Princess. A visitor named Jocelyn Gordon Whitehead asked him about the challenge, and Houdini bragged that he could take a lot without injury. At one point Whitehead took Houdini by surprise and delivered several powerful punches to his midriff before he had a chance to prepare.

Houdini performed that evening and the next few days in extreme pain. What he didn't know is that Whitehead had ruptured his appendix, which spread infection through his abdomen. By the time he finally consented to see a doctor two days later in another town, it was too late. Houdini died on Halloween 1926.

After a long history as a vaudeville and Burlesque theatre, then a movie theatre, the Princess building went downhill, suffered a devastating fire in 2002, and finally stood abandoned for years before it was demolished. It's location is now the site of the Hotel Birks Montreal.

During its years as a movie house, the Princess was the scene of several dramatic appearances by a specter people identified as Houdini. He was formally attired in a cape and top hat, as if he was going out on the town.

The Princess Theatre is long gone, but the ghostly rumors persist.

ST. JAMES'S THEATRE, LONDON

Here's one from London: St. James's Theatre, which was best known for presenting the world premieres of several Oscar Wilde plays, notably his masterpiece *The Importance of Being Earnest*. Perhaps owing to the support shown by the theatre in the years of his greatest success, Wilde was said to haunt St. James's. A figure closely resembling Wilde at his most elegant appears to workers and visitors when they are by themselves. His hauntings started soon after his death in 1900 at age forty-six, and by the 1920s, those who wanted to speak with him directly organized a séance at the theatre. During the proceedings, a hand is said to have materialized and written Wilde's name.

St. James's was demolished in 1957 and the author of *The Picture of Dorian Grey* came no more.

PHANTASMAGORIA

Showbiz and the supernatural were made for each other. Popular 1960s media theorist Marshall McLuhan considered theatre to be generally a "hot" medium because of the intensity of the information being conveyed on multiple levels.

But audiences of the eighteenth and nineteenth centuries knew nothing about all that. They did know, however, that they loved a good scare that would send a chill galloping down their spine like a glissando on a piano. And that was the inspiration for one of the great ghost traditions that has vanished (or morphed): the phantasmagoria.

We discussed Pepper's Ghost in chapter 7, but that was just the tip of the ghostberg as far as pre-twentieth-century spooky special effects were concerned. The practitioners of these traveling horror shows used a number of primitive (but highly effective) technologies to scare the bejesus out of people. But the most important tool in their toolchests was the audience itself: an audience that was innocent, inexperienced, and not yet jaded. It's rare to find such an audience today in an age of mass media, but they were plentiful during the golden age of phantasmagorias, and really easy to frighten.

Audiences would gather in darkened theatres, usually decorated with cobwebs and cutouts of bats and such, and watch as images of devils, skeletons, ghouls, witches, monsters, cannibals, the tortures of Hell, and, yes, especially *ghosts* appeared before them. These horrors were projected onto curtains, walls, screens, or even onto smoke. The images came from a primitive type of projector, one known as a camera obscura and another called a magic lantern. These worked not much differently from mid-twentieth-century slide projectors, and, in fact, helped give rise to their higher-tech descendants. There were no moving pictures yet during the nineteenth-century boom time of phantasmagorias, but the operators would use multiple magic lanterns and roll them around on wheels to make the nightmares seem like they were moving. The images would be accompanied by spooky sound effects created backstage, and sometimes accompanied by a live performance by actors costumed as demons and phantasms.

In the end, pure phantasmagorias died out because modern audiences simply began to see so many special effects in movies and TV that they lost that innocent, joyously gullible sense of wonder and amazement. Nowadays, people have seen it all before. The time is gone when a still image of the devil projected on a screen in a darkened room could strike genuine fear in people's lives and souls. Classic phantasmagorias that drew shrieks and prompted fainting and seizures now would likely prompt chuckles—or yawns.

By no means does that mean the public's appetite for shock and horror isn't still just as sharp. Phantasmagoria today is satisfied by increasingly violent and explicit horror movies, usually released around Halloween, and online role-playing games like *Darkwood* and *Call of*

Cthulu. There was even a horror-themed video game in the 1990s titled *Phantasmagoria.* Props for the callback.

Stage phantasmagorias live on in small-scale Halloween-season attractions, like haunted houses or haunted forests and even some haunted theatres. Actors dress up as zombies, mummies, witches, and so on, and use the usual sound effects and dramatic lighting as they jump from darkened corners to scare the pants off visitors looking for a thrill (or a laugh).

A special favorite is the one they hold each year in Sleepy Hollow, a village in the town of Mount Pleasant, New York, reenacting the ride of the Headless Horseman from Washington Irving's story "The Legend of Sleepy Hollow."

In his book of essays, *Danse Macabre,* author Stephen King posits that people read and attend ghost and horror stories, not just to run that chill down their spine, but to measure their courage. After an especially grisly or terrifying moment they can say to themselves, "I was able to handle that," and feel better about themselves.

So how are you doing so far?

13

LITERARY GHOST STORIES

Peace, break thee off; look where it comes again!

—*Hamlet*

Despite everything you've read so far, the most common type of ghost to be seen in the theatre is a fictional one on stage. And there have been a lot of them. Many plays of the past—and a surprising number of ones from the present, including several recent Pulitzer Prize winners—feature ghosts as characters. Here is a tiny sampling of some of the most interesting and/or popular ones you may wish to track down.

THE PHANTOM OF THE OPERA

Perhaps the most famous theatre ghost is not actually a ghost at all. The Phantom in *The Phantom of the Opera*, appears and disappears like a ghost, but he is very much alive—a facially disfigured musical genius who lives in a secret grotto deep beneath the Paris Opera and wears a half-mask to conceal his hideous visage from the cruel world. He knows all the secret passages around the opera house, which enables him to give the appearance of materializing and dematerializing. This allows him to frighten the management into letting him call the shots about casting and repertoire choices. But, in reality, calling himself a "ghost" is just another one of his masks.

PULITZER PRIZE WINNERS WITH GHOSTS

Ghosts may be pooh-poohed in the world at large, but there is a long history of ghosts being taken very seriously in the world of theatre. Why not? They are so dramatic. And modern science has scarcely affected that. Some of the most lauded of recent plays involved ghostly visits. Look at some of the Pulitzer Prize–winning dramas: *Angels in America*, *Our Town*, *The Piano Lesson*, *Proof*, and many others feature ghostly encounters as key plot points.

Ghosts are often depicted as having wisdom and perspective unavailable to the living. In Margaret Edson's *Wit* (1995), Dr. Vivian Bearing, a university professor of English, specializes in the poems of John Donne, author of "Death Be Not Proud." Many of his poems were about death, which adds a desperate significance for Vivian when she learns she is dying of cancer. In the play's final scene, after she dies, she returns as a ghost who has achieved transcendent insight and at last truly understands Donne's work.

And Pulitzer-winning musicals are scarcely exempt. *Next to Normal* is a 2009 musical about Diana, a woman whose mental health has continued to slide downhill since the death of her young son Gabe. Diana suffers hallucinations of seeing the ghostlike Gabe as a grown young man and interacting with him. In the deceptively sweet song "I Dreamed a Dance," couched as a lilting waltz orchestrated to sound like a pretty music box playing a haunting lullaby, Diana dances happily with Gabe's ghost—and tells him that she's willing to kill herself so she can be reunited with him and dance with him forever. She subsequently attempts to do just that. Gabe's ghost lives in Diana's mind and becomes the kind of spirit who tries to lure the living into the next world.

Sunday in the Park with George by James Lapine and Stephen Sondheim imagines the story behind George Seurat's 1886 masterpiece of pointillist painting, *Sunday Afternoon on the Island of La Grande Jatte.* Act 1 dramatizes Seurat's conflicts with the world around him, including his girlfriend Dot, who leaves him (even though she is pregnant) because of his obsession with his work. In return, Seurat immortalizes her as the dominant figure in the painting. Act 2 jumps forward a century to show the similar conflicts faced by Seurat's great-grandson, also an artist named George. As his internal conflict comes to a head, young George is visited by the ghost of Dot, who shares wisdom she gathered from his ancestor, especially the advice that he should be true to his own inner voice and "keep moving on." Doing so, she closes this unfinished chapter in her life and begins a new chapter for George.

HAMLET

All the best shows have a ghost. Shakespeare knew it, and that's why he wrote so many into some of his greatest plays.

That includes what many consider his greatest masterpiece, *Hamlet.* The play opens with a pair of terrified guards at the Danish castle of Elsinore who have seen a ghost each of the two previous nights, a ghost they know well: the old king, who recently died under suspicious circumstances. Word of the apparition has come to Horatio, close friend of the king's son, Prince Hamlet. Horatio, too, sees the ghost and runs to fetch Hamlet.

Even with the primitive stagecraft of 1609, the appearance of the ghost at the Globe Theatre was surprising and terrifying. The dead king speaks to his son, telling him that he died unnaturally. He was murdered by his uncle, who now sits on the throne and has taken Hamlet's mother as his wife. The ghost demands that young Hamlet avenge his death, setting all the action of the tragedy in motion. Ghosts are fun to watch and fun to play, and tradition says that the role of the ghost king was originated by none other than the Bard himself.

MACBETH

Shakespeare wrote plays in pretty much every genre from rom-coms (*Love's Labours Lost*) to costume epics (*Antony and Cleopatra*) to slapstick (*The Merry Wives of Windsor*), to history (the *Henry* plays), to sword-and-sorcery adventures (*The Tempest*) to revenge dramas (*Othello*). But he was especially adept at horror, as evidenced by *Titus Andronicus* and one of his most popular dramas, the supposedly cursed *Macbeth*.

Macbeth is a Scottish nobleman who has just won a war for his king, Duncan, with the help of his comrade in arms, Banquo. On the way home from the triumphant battle, Macbeth and Banquo are met by three witches who have portentous prophecies for them both. They tell Macbeth that someday he will be king of Scotland. When Banquo asks to know his fortune, they tell him that his descendants—but not he—will also be kings of Scotland.

This sets the two friends at odds, and leads to terrible violence. Macbeth, urged by his ambitious wife, murders Duncan and seizes the throne. He then plots to murder Banquo as well, to prevent the witches' prophesy from coming true. More murders, including women and children, follow as Macbeth tries to solidify his accursed hold on the throne.

This blood-drenched story is deeply haunted. When contemplating the assassination, Macbeth sees a ghostly dagger floating in front of him. He wonders if this ghostly object is real or just a figment of his imagination—a "dagger of the mind." It's a question that goes to the heart of the ghost experience at large:

> *Is this a dagger which I see before me,*
> *The handle toward my hand? Come, let me clutch thee.*
> *I have thee not, and yet I see thee still.*
> *Art thou not, fatal vision, sensible*
> *To feeling as to sight? or art thou but*
> *A dagger of the mind, a false creation,*
> *Proceeding from the heat-oppressed brain?*
> *I see thee yet, in form as palpable*
> *As this which now I draw.*

After assassinating the king, Macbeth's castle produces supernatural groans that cause Macbeth and his Lady to startle in fright. Nature herself seems to recoil at the crime. The character of Lennox notes,

> *The night has been chaotic.*
> *The wind blew down through the chimneys where we were sleeping.*
> *People are saying they heard cries of grief in the air,*
> *Strange screams of death, and terrible voices predicting catastrophes*

That will usher in a woeful new age.
The owl made noise all night.
Some people say that the earth shook as if it had a fever.

Later, at a feast to celebrate his coronation, the gory ghost of Banquo materializes as an accusatory guest. Only Macbeth can see him, but his over-the-top reaction makes the other guests suspect his guilty conscience. Are these spirits actual restless souls? Or are they purely the result of his uneasy imagination?

And the play's supernatural history doesn't stop there. The script itself is said to be haunted. Productions of the popular tragedy have been accompanied by more than their share of mishaps, accidents, and the periodic gruesome death. As a result, the witchcraft-imbued play is commonly regarded as cursed. Uttering the title aloud inside a theatre (by some accounts, saying it *anywhere*) is strictly verboten. It's okay to refer to it euphemistically as "The Scottish Play," but in its original form? Never!

But sometimes it happens. So, what to do?

According to the Royal Shakespeare Company (on its official website, no less), to undo the curse, leave the theatre immediately, close the stage door, turn around three times, then spit and utter a swear word out loud. After this ritual is performed you must knock on the stage door and ask to be readmitted.

In another form, de-*Macbeth*ing can be performed inside the theatre. It also involves spinning three times. But, in this less-sanitary variation on the ritual, you must spit over your shoulder and curse each time you spin. You then must speak a line from a different Shakespeare play to invoke the counterspell.

Then again, of course, theatre people could just stop doing the play. The problem is it's so well written and the characters so juicy that it will always attract actors at the top of their game, willing to take the risk. The Internet Broadway Database lists no fewer than forty-eight Broadway productions of the play since the middle of the nineteenth century, including four since 2000, and one as recently as 2022 (with Daniel Craig). Countless more are done across the United States and internationally.

Some productions have tried to combat the curse head on. The November 2013 Lincoln Center production with Ethan Hawke as Macbeth had a set by Scott Pask that incorporated a mandala consisting of two circles, a pentagram, and three heptagons, all labeled with the name of God and His angels. The design was based on "The Seal of God's Truth," created in 1582 by Dr. John Dee, a mathematician, astronomer, and scholar who was a member of the court of Queen Elizabeth I. Dr. Dee claimed to have been instructed in its design through direct communication with angels. The mandala was painted on the Beaumont Theatre stage and the entire production was played directly upon it.

Production stage manager Tripp Phillips reported that the show was uncharacteristically trouble-free.

BLITHE SPIRIT/HIGH SPIRITS

Perhaps the best-known attempt to play a ghost story for comedy is *Blithe Spirit*, English author Noël Coward's 1941 script about Charles Condomine, a writer who arranges to take part in a séance as research for an upcoming novel. He is alarmed to discover that the ceremony accidentally calls up the ghost of his dead wife, Elvira. Horrified at first and later annoyed, Condomine also discovers that he rather likes having his sexy and charismatic late spouse around the house—though the situation creates understandable conflict with his comparatively dull new wife, Ruth. However, it quickly appears that Elvira is scheming to kill Condomine so they can be together forever. At the end, Elvira, Condomine, *and* Ruth all wind up together as ghosts, and seem quite merry about it indeed.

Coward legendarily dashed out the play in less that week on a sojourn to Wales, where he had fled after the Nazi blitz damaged his London home and office. The timing of the story wasn't lost on Coward, who believed the story would strike a chord in wartime audiences who were facing death on a daily basis. He worried that the lighthearted approach might be perceived as being in bad taste, but ultimately *Blithe Spirit* turned out to be not so much a comedy about death, but a comforting fable about life that continues *after* death. Leave it to Coward to concoct a story that uses ghosts, not to terrify, but to comfort the living.

The show opened in the West End just six weeks later and eventually became, for a time, London's longest-running production. It was also made into a popular film, starring Rex Harrison as Condomine.

In 1964, the play was adapted as a Broadway musical with book, music, and lyrics by Hugh Martin and Timothy Gray. The musical featured Tammy Grimes as Elvira, and Beatrice Lillie as Madame Arcati, the medium who conducts the show's seances. Angela Lansbury played Arcati in a 2009 Broadway revival of the straight play, earning her fifth Tony Award in the process. Some ghost stories are just timeless.

ANGELS IN AMERICA

Ghosts of several kinds prowl through Tony Kushner's landmark drama *Angels in America*. A combination of politics on earth and in heaven in the early days of the AIDS epidemic, the drama allows fictional characters to interact with historical ones. One of the central characters, Prior Walter, who is suffering from AIDS, hallucinates a visit from the ghosts of two ancestors, a thirteenth-century serf and a seventeenth-century aristocrat, both also named Prior. The prior Priors act as prophets, foretelling that the current Prior will soon be visited by a literal angel from heaven.

On the historical side is Roy Cohn, the ferociously conservative lawyer who was a right-hand man to anti-Communist witch-hunter Sen. Joseph McCarthy. Cohn is also a deeply closeted gay man who eventually dies of AIDS. Also facing disbarment and seeing his old allies turning their backs on him, Cohn collapses in the play and is visited by the ghost of Soviet spy Ethel Rosenberg, who has unfinished business with him. She blames Cohn for prosecuting her and pressing for her controversial execution. Rosenberg gets revenge of a sort by delivering the news that Cohn has indeed been disbarred, but then she comforts him in his final moments of life by singing a lullaby—in Russian. She also guides another character in reciting the Kaddish—the Jewish prayer for the dead—over the dead Cohn.

OUR TOWN

On the other hand, one of the tenderest and most heartbreaking ghost scenes in all literature occurs in the 1938 Thornton Wilder play *Our Town*.

A deceptively artless depiction of a few years in the simple lives of these simple characters in the small town of Grovers Corners, New Hampshire, *Our Town*, winds up asking profound questions about the fundamentals of human existence—and what comes after.

In act 2, the play takes us on a visit to the afterlife. Emily Gibbs, a young mother we've followed since her own childhood back in act 1, has died in childbirth. Her spirit arrives at the town cemetery where she reunites with her deceased mother-in-law and other friends and neighbors who have passed on. But passed on to where? Good question. Even they're not sure. They sit, waiting for something to summon them to an indefinable beyond.

Emily isn't ready to go, and still feels connected with the living world. She asks the Stage Manager, the godlike narrator of the play who is also able to start and stop the action, to relive one day of her life. The Stage Manager reluctantly suggests that she pick a day, any day, an unremarkable day. Emily chooses her twelfth birthday. But after reliving it for just a few minutes, she begs to return to her grave. But first . . .

"Wait! One more look. Goodbye, goodbye, world. Goodbye, Grover's Corners . . . Mamma and Papa. Goodbye to clocks ticking . . . and Mama's sunflowers. And food and coffee. And new-ironed dresses and hot baths . . . and sleeping and waking up. Oh, earth, you're too wonderful for anybody to realize you."

She asks the Stage Manager, "Do any human beings ever realize life while they live it—every, every minute?"

The Stage Manager answers, "No. Saints and poets maybe . . . they do, some."

You might add that the ones who feel the keenest sense of the living world, are those who have been forever removed from it like Emily— the ghosts of the once-living.

Wilder has the Stage Manager observe, "We all know that something is eternal. And it ain't houses and it ain't names, and it ain't earth, and it ain't even the stars . . . everybody knows in their bones that something is eternal, and that something has to do with human beings. All the greatest people ever lived have been telling us that for five thousand years and yet you'd be surprised how people are always losing hold of it. There's something way down deep that's eternal about every human being."

CAROUSEL

Rodgers and Hammerstein's many wonderful musicals are filled with flights of lyrical fancy—brooks laughing as they trip and fall over stones on their way, and such. But most of their stories keep their feet firmly on the ground as far as supernatural subjects go. With one exception. In the 1945 *Carousel*, based on Ferenc Molnar's 1909 *Liliom*, tough-guy carnival barker Billy Bigelow is desperate to provide for his young wife Julie when he learns that she is going to have a baby. He's never had to think about anyone but himself, and the sudden new responsibility drives him to commit a robbery, since he is convinced that it's the only way to make a lot of money fast.

The problem is, Billy is an amateur thief. He bungles the stickup, takes a bullet in the chest, and dies in Julie's arms. But his story doesn't end there. We see Billy in the afterlife, trying to bluster his way past a Godlike character known as the Starkeeper to get into heaven. But the Starkeeper has seen plenty of mugs like Billy before. Nevertheless, he perceives a bit of good in Billy and gives him a chance to redeem himself and complete his unfinished business of preparing the child he never got to see, the now-teenaged Louise, for life.

The Starkeeper sends Billy back to earth as a ghostlike figure who can appear to the living at will. After a few clumsy attempts to connect with Louise, including offering her a star he stole from heaven, Billy smacks her hand—a smack she later describes (controversially) as feeling like a kiss. He then sings the soaring R&H anthem "You'll Never Walk Alone," and you get the sense that this ghost has finally done something selfless and effective, thereby redeeming his uncouth soul.

THE WEIR

One of the creepiest and, indeed, sickest ghost plays is Conor McPherson's 1997 *The Weir*, about friends who gather in an Irish country pub to swap spooky stories in an attempt to intimidate a visiting big-city woman from Dublin. Instead, as the stories get creepier, it's the woman who throws a scare into *them*.

The workman Jim tells about the time he was digging a grave at a local cemetery when he was approached by a man who told him he was digging in the wrong spot. The man led Jim to another grave, that of a young girl whose pretty picture adorned the gravestone. It becomes apparent that the mysterious man was the ghost of a child molester who was seeking to continue his abominations on children, even after death.

Brr.

SHINING CITY

Another creepy Conor McPherson play is the less-known *Shining City*. It waits with dreadful patience to scare your pants off. The main character is coping with the trauma of seeing a horrifying ghost. Everyone around him spends the entire play convincing him that what he saw was merely a hallucination, a product of some deep-seated emotional issue. In the play's last moment, the man shuts a door and behind the door is an utterly terrifying specter! The audience sees it for only a moment before blackout, but it always prompts gasps and screams.

AN INSPECTOR CALLS

Many ghosts return to get even for a wrong that was done to them, but the wraith in J. B. Priestley's *An Inspector Calls*, haunts the corrupt upper-class Birling family on behalf of someone else.

The family is sharing a pleasant dinner when a mysterious Inspector Goole arrives on their doorstep. He's come to investigate the suicide of a young working-class woman named Eva Smith. Conditioned, perhaps, by Agatha Christie's murder mysteries, the audience may expect Goole to find the individual responsible for her death, but it gradually becomes apparent that everyone in the family had a hand in driving Eva Smith to her final act of self-destruction—one family member by causing Eva to lose her job, another by failing to help Eva, and so on.

After Goole leaves, the family decides to check his credentials—only to learn that there is no one by that name on the local police force. They have been visited, accused, and convicted by an avenging spirit.

LES MISÉRABLES

A thirteen-letter title is said to be bad luck in the theatre—though it doesn't seem to have harmed the musical *Les Misérables*, one of the longest-running plays in many cities and countries where it has appeared. Few hard-core fans would think of the show as a ghost story per se, but there is a stirring ghostly moment in the show's finale. The now-elderly Jean Valjean is on the verge of death and makes his peace with Cosette, the girl he raised from childhood, by sharing a letter that reveals the truth about her mother, Fantine.

As Valjean slips into unconsciousness, Fantine's spirit and that of the maiden Eponine appear at his side to guide him to heaven. They are joined by the souls of all the people who died earlier on the barricades. In the reprise of "Do You Hear the People Sing," they assure Valjean that freedom from all earthly tyranny awaits him in the next world as a reward for his steadfastness. These ghosts are the opposite of frightening. They are filled with reassurance and love.

HOW I LEARNED TO DRIVE

Paula Vogel's *How I Learned to Drive* is not overtly a ghost play. It is a memory play about a young woman named Li'l Bit who comes to grips with the fact that her uncle used a series of driving lessons as a pretext to sexually abuse her when she was a teen. The play goes beyond the fact of the abuse to explore questions of power and control, and also the factors that may have led her middle-aged uncle to damage his niece, his marriage, and ultimately himself.

Driving itself becomes a metaphor for freedom in the drama, and all the threads come together in the last moments when Li'l Bit frees herself from the past and prepares to drive away—only to see the ghost of her uncle in the car's rear view mirror. Perhaps this ghost is only a memory. But it has the dramatic heft and impact of a ghost.

WHAT'S WRONG WITH THIS PICTURE?

One of the oddest ghost stories of the stage is found in Donald Margulies's 1994 black comedy *What's Wrong with This Picture?* As the play opens, Mort is mourning his beloved wife, Shirley, who choked to death on a chunk of moo shu pork. As he and his son Artie try to grapple with her loss, they're stunned to see her suddenly and without explanation return from the grave and resume cooking, cleaning, redecorating their house, and wrapping up a bunch of unfinished business.

However, it soon becomes clear that retail resurrections are not in the cards, and the world has already moved on. Realizing that she's overstayed her welcome on this plane of existence, Shirley reluctantly returns to her grave.

THE BRONX BOMBERS

Relatively few stage plays have dealt with the world of sports, and fewer still of these have a ghostly dimension, but Eric Simonson's 2014 drama *The Bronx Bombers* boasts both. These ghosts are helpful ghosts whose attachment to one of the greatest teams in professional sports—the New York Yankees—brings them back from the afterlife.

The play is set in 1977 when Yanks coach Yogi Berra is trying to deal with a corrosive rivalry between two of his star players, Billy Martin and Reggie Jackson. That night, he dreams that he's visited by the ghosts of former Yankees greats, from Babe Ruth and Lou Gehrig to Joe DiMaggio and Mickey Mantle—and even the spirit of future star Derek Jeter. They share their collective wisdom and help him to guide the team back to championship form.

RAGTIME

Just as some ghosts appear to be trying to settle unfinished business, some literary ghosts are introduced to complete a story arc, or to place a posthumous blessing (or curse) on how the story has come out.

The musical *Ragtime*, by Stephen Flaherty, Lynn Ahrens, and Terrence McNally, based on the 1975 novel of the same name by E. L. Doctorow, dramatizes the untimely deaths of its two African American main characters Coalhouse Walker Jr. and his wife, Sarah. Sarah is beaten to death by police when she tries to approach a vice presidential candidate for help after racist firefighters destroy Coalhouse's car. In revenge, Coalhouse is driven to take over the Morgan Library in New York City and threatens to blow it up if he doesn't get justice. After long negotiations he is persuaded to surrender peaceably—only to be cut down by police bullets.

Both return as spirits in the final moments of the play to watch their son growing up in a country they hope will offer him a better chance than they got. These optimistic ghosts don't just provide an easy happy twist to the ending. They are designed to be aspirational and inspirational. They prick our consciences about building the better world they deserve and that drive the "Wheels of a Dream" they sing about.

"DA"

Hugh Leonard's Tony Award-winning 1973 play *"Da"* tells the story of an Irish writer named Charlie who inherits his boyhood home—which happens to come with a veritable squad of brogued ghosts, mainly deceased family members, but also including the ghost of his own younger self—shades of *Follies*.

However the most important ghost in this play is the title character, Charlie's late dad, whom Charlie always addressed as "Da." Charlie gets to ask his father questions that so many children never get to ask their parents before it's too late. But Charlie gets the opportunity to discover his "Da" for who he was, a simple but flawed man. In life, Charlie had to leave him behind because he was embarrassed and angry at his father, despite the fact that he truly loved him. He always wanted to bring "Da" along, but his father would never accompany him.

Now, father and son decided to bury the hatchet posthumously, and when the time comes for Charlie to return to London his "Da" finally decides to go along with him.

This is a rare example of a story in which the ghost and the haunted person display no terror and establish a working relationship, of sorts. If anything, the living person is haunting the ghost here, trying to hound him into a relationship he was never capable of having when alive.

THÉRÈSE RAQUIN/THOU SHALT NOT

A classic story of an avenging ghost can be found in Émile Zola's 1867 novel *Thérèse Raquin*, a lurid story that has been adapted to the stage (and film) several times, including a 2001 musical version with a score by Harry Connick Jr. and libretto by David Thompson. All of them tell the story of Thérèse, a passionate woman in an unhappy marriage. She takes a lover, Laurent, and the two of them plot to murder her husband, which they accomplish by shoving him out of a rowboat to drown.

The abrupt end to his life and the desire for revenge from beyond the grave causes the husband to haunt the couple's bedroom. Thérèse and Laurent marry, but every time they try to make love, the ghost of her husband appears and drives them apart. Terror and guilt overwhelm the couple, and the ghost gets his revenge when they both commit suicide.

THE PIANO LESSON

One of the greatest and most underappreciated of modern dramas is *The Piano Lesson*, part of the playwright August Wilson's Century Cycle of ten plays about black life in America during each decade of the twentieth century. Set in 1936 Pittsburgh, Pennsylvania, *The Piano Lesson* tells the story of the Charles family and their struggle to move into the future while grappling with their past.

The Piano Lesson is also a ghost story.

The central piece of scenery is a gorgeous 137-year-old, upright piano, decorated with African totems and motifs. The piano holds special significance for the family because it was once traded for an ancestor who was a slave to the Sutter Family. Boy Willie, recently released from prison, comes home with the intention of selling the piano to get money to buy the Sutter family land where his family was once slaves. It is gradually revealed that the last living Sutter was recently killed by falling—or being pushed—into a well.

Sutter's ghost appears again and again in the Charles household. But he is far from the only ghost fluttering through the darkness. Mention is made of the Ghosts of the Yellow Dog, which represent the family's long line of ancestors, who are blamed at one point for Sutter's death, plus the ghost of the more recently dead grandparents who clung to the piano as a replacement for holding onto the full legacy of their family history.

The ghosts in *The Piano Lesson* are ghosts of individuals, but they are also collective ghosts who form a history and an imperative for their still-living descendants.

FIDDLER ON THE ROOF, THE ADDAMS FAMILY, RUDDIGORE

There are many prominent examples of ghosts used for comic effect. One of the best-known examples is the ghost of Fruma-Sarah in *Fiddler on the Roof*. In the scene "Tevye's Dream," the main character, Tevye the Milkman, has given his daughter Tzeitl permission to marry her sweetheart, penniless Motel the Tailor. The problem is that Tevye is henpecked by his wife Golde and they had previously arranged a marriage for Tzeitl to the well-off butcher Lazar Wolf, whom Golde considers to be a good catch for a girl with no dowry.

To overcome what he expects will be his wife's hectoring opposition, Tevye makes up a dream in which he is visited by two ghosts,

Golde's grandmother, who says that Tzeitl was meant to marry Motel, not Lazar. But she is then joined by a second ghost, Lazar Wolf's first wife, Fruma-Sarah, who warns that she will strangle Tzeitl if she dares to take her place in Lazar's bed. Impressed and frightened by Tevye's made-up dream, Golde agrees to the change in grooms. Tevye breathes a sigh of relief. He's off the hook.

That's far from the only instance of using ghosts to provoke a spell of nervous laughter. The musical adaptation of *The Addams Family* treats the ghosts of the family ancestors as still-functioning members of the family. They serve as a singing-dancing (stiffly) chorus in the opening number, "When You're an Addams," and help to establish the topsy-turvy, horror-as-normal Addams world.

Similarly, in the Gilbert and Sullivan operetta *Ruddigore*, the ghosts of the Murgatroyd ancestors emerge from their stern portraits that line walls of Ruddigore Castle and try to help their hapless descendant, Ruthven Murgatroyd, break an ancient curse that requires the baronets to commit a new crime every day or die a horrible death ("Painted Emblems of a Race"). The ghosts are deeply and comically disappointed in the quality of Ruthven's crimes, including filing a false tax return but eventually help him to find a typically Gilbertian twist of logic to end the curse.

I HATE HAMLET

In Paul Rudnick's *I Hate Hamlet,* a young television actor named Andrew is faced with the terrifying challenge of having to play the title role of Hamlet in an upcoming Central Park production. As Andrew deals with that (and his girlfriend), he is visited by the ghost of temperamental real-life master actor John Barrymore. The egotistical thespian, who was known as "The Great Profile" in his heyday, proceeds to coach Andrew—none too gently, either—in how to play the role. The scenario is usually played strictly for comedy, though the original Broadway production featured Nichol Williamson, who did not get along with his costar Evan Handler. Handler left the production after Williamson injured him in what was supposed to be a pretend sword fight. Luckily, he didn't become a ghost himself.

KAIDAN

Most of our examples here are found in the Western canon. But many other theatrical traditions traffic in many kinds of ghosts. The Japanese, in particular, delight in ghost stories or *kaidan*. Most interesting are that nation's Noh plays, which have a subgenre dealing specifically with *Shura-mono*, warrior ghosts. Divided into several sub-subgenres, they exist to fill in backstory about battles that occur before or during the action of the play, or to tell the stories of their lives and noble endings. Some are on a mission to find an object or person irrevocably lost. The Japanese tradition of Kabuki theatre explores its own family of ghosts, known as *Yūrei*.

Tokaido Yotsuya Kaidan is based on supposedly real-life characters—a man who murders his devoted wife, Oiwa, so he can be with his lover. Oiwa returns from the dead as a ghost to wreak vengeance on him and his new love. The play is, in its way, the *Macbeth* of Japan, in that it is said to be cursed and haunted by the ghost of the real Oiwa, who, according to historian Frances Dilworth, harasses any "who dare to perform in the plays and movies inspired by her life. . . . In order to appease her restless spirit, actors visit her grave to pay their respects before embarking on their gruesome task."

BEETLEJUICE

Based on the 1988 Tim Burton film of the same title, the Broadway musical *Beetlejuice* tells the story of a young couple who buy an old house only to discover that it is crawling with ghosts, especially one named Beetlejuice (after the star Betelgeuse) who befriends them because he is on a mission. In order to be released to move on to the Great Beyond, Beetlejuice needs to finds a living person to say his name three times. One of the most memorable aspects of the production is the wildly creative ghostly effects credited to Jeremy Chernick, set designer David Korins, and "Magic & Illusion Designer" Michael Weber.

Beetlejuice originally ran 366 performances from April 29, 2019, to March 10, 2020, when it closed, along with the rest of American live theatre, due to the COVID-19 pandemic. The show had been scheduled to close on its own in June 2020, so its theatre, the Winter Garden, went to a revival of *The Music Man*. But early in 2022 it was announced that *Beetlejuice* would rise from the dead and resume its run at the Marquis Theatre in Times Square. The ghost show found itself seizing a life after death.

Another recent show that skillfully deploys a dazzling selection of high-tech and low-tech magical ghostly effects is the Tony Award–winning *Harry Potter and the Cursed Child*.

PLAYS ABOUT THE AFTERLIFE

There is a whole subgenre of plays that offer glimpses of what awaits in the afterlife, usually in unexpected and allegorical ways.

Sutton Vane's widely copied 1923 drama *Outward Bound* shows seven travelers aboard an ocean liner, but they have no idea how they got there or where they are headed. As they get to know one another, it gradually dawns on them that they have, in fact, died and are traveling toward the afterlife. A mysterious Examiner who has been chatting them up is revealed as the entity who will judge their lives and decide whether they will dock in heaven or at a considerably more torrid destination.

French philosopher Jean-Paul Sartre coined the widely misunderstood aphorism, "Hell is other people," in his 1944 existentialist play *Huis clos* (*No Exit*). It shows what happens to three people who find themselves trapped in a room with no door. As in *Outward Bound*, they gradually come to understand that they are dead, but in this case their spirits have already been consigned to hell, which is this room, and they will spend eternity sniping at each other.

A more modern and fanciful twist on this theme is Bruce Jay Friedman's 1970 play *Steambath*, in which a spa-style towels-and-all steambath is proposed as the waiting room for the next world. The "customers" in the steambath know they are dead, and explain the setup to a newcomer, who is frantic to return to life. Instead of being uplifted or awestruck, the ghostly bathers seem still obsessed with the petty problems of their former lives, even as they wait for the voice of God to summon them into the next room—whatever that might hold.

A CHRISTMAS CAROL

We conclude our barely-scratched-the-surface tour through fictional stage ghosts with the most widely produced, most widely seen, and probably even most-loved of all (whatever your religion or political persuasion): *A Christmas Carol*, based on Charles Dickens's 1843 novella of the same title.

The ghosts include Jacob Marley; the Ghosts of Christmas Past, Present, and Yet to Come; Ignorance; and Want. Each of them is a highly unusual ghost, and of a very different kind.

First of all, except for Marley, these are ghosts, not of individual human beings, but of holidays and even general human conditions. And they are not there to make you jump in fear, but to teach a powerful lesson to the central character, the iconic skinflint Ebenezer Scrooge, whose name itself has become a synonym for cheapskate. These lessons are designed to save Scrooge's soul from the "weary long chain" that his dead partner Marley, usually shown as a traditional human-derived spook, must suffer through eternity, presumably in Hell.

Three main conceptual ghosts—the Spirit of Christmas Past, the Spirit of Christmas Present, and the Spirit of Christmas Yet to Come—are untraditional ghosts in other ways as well. They are not tied to a single place and are not locked into performing the same action over and over. These are ghosts on a mission. They show Scrooge scenes from throughout his life, dramatizing how he got where he is, how he grew so greedy, and what could happen to him if he doesn't change his ways.

In an interesting reversal, during their time with Scrooge, the Spirits become "real," and the real people of the real world become merely shadows.

Dickens calls the ghosts "Spirits," perhaps to show they are something more than mere revenants. One of the spirits shows Scrooge yet a further set of spirits, two hideous, emaciated child ghosts who embody Ignorance and Want. Their plight has a powerful effect on Scrooge—and on us.

There have been literally hundreds of stage adaptations of this story over the eighteen decades since it was published in December 1843, including the first one, in London in February 1844. By March of 1844 there were seven more adaptations on the West End boards. Read those dates again. Some are literal enactments of Dickens's tale, such as Patrick Stewart's Broadway recitation of the entire original story from memory, with the lone actor adjusting his voice and carriage to play every character.

There have been gender-reversed *Christmas Carols*, modernized *Christmas Carols*, animated cartoon *Christmas Carols*, *The Muppet Christmas Carol*, *Mr. Magoo's Christmas Special*, a Mickey Mouse *Christmas Carol*, a Bugs Bunny *Christmas Carol*, a "Family Guy" *Christmas Carol*, the story of the writing of *A Christmas Carol*, one recent mashup of "A Christmas Carol" and Sherlock Holmes, titled *A Sherlock Carol*, and an endless cornucopia of musical adaptations for stage, film, screen, web, and social media.

What gives the story—and its many ghosts—its special power? These are ghosts formed out of the collective spirit of a great holiday, a great moment in religious history. They draw their power from their proximity to Christmas, even though neither Jesus nor any other deity is directly mentioned, even in the original story, not to mention the many secularized versions since then. Dickens's ghosts are there to instruct, to reveal, and to save the soul of an individual specially chosen, it seems, because he appears to be irrevocably in the clutches of Satan.

These ghosts aren't just "friendly" to the living. They are their last hope.

EPILOGUE

So now you've learned of the many types of theatre ghosts, their behavior, their habits, their peculiarities, their tragedies and, in some cases, their pleasures.

Let's consider for a moment: What if 99 percent of the world is right and there are no such things as ghosts?

Well then, what are all these people seeing? Are they all just hallucinating? Are ghosts just figments of their imaginations? Are they just seeing what they want to see? Are these monsters from the id?

And why do people from different times and places, people who may not know each other and may not have discussed the vision together—why do they see the same things?

For many people, their childhood interest in theatre grows into a lifelong obsession and a lifelong delight. Those people will find comfort in the fact that, for no small number of their fellow theatre lovers, the delight—and the obsession—seems to persist even beyond the span of a lifetime, beyond the confines of the theatre, and beyond the boundaries of the world we know.

Have you ever had a ghostly experience inside a theatre? Not something you heard about—something that actually happened to you, or you actually witnessed. If so, please share! Send your stories to ViagasGhost@gmail.com.

Citations by Chapter

PREFACE

Charles J. Adams, *Philadelphia Ghost Stories* (Reading, PA: Exeter House Books, 2012).

Frank Rich, *Ghost Light: A Memoir* (New York: Random House, 2000).

Thornton Wilder, *Our Town: A Play in Three Acts* (New York: Harper Perennial Modern Classics: A Reissue Edition, 2020).

Stephen Sondheim (lyrics) and Arthur Laurents (libretto), *Romeo and Juliet and West Side Story* (New York: Laurel Leaf/Random House, 1965).

CHAPTER ONE: THE NEW AMSTERDAM THEATRE

"From $2.75 to $4,000 Weekly as a Movie Star," *Pittsburg Press*, February 4, 1931, p. 19.

"An Ugly Ending for the World's Most Beautiful Girl," *Journal of Yesterday*, October 22, 2020.

Michelle Vogel, *Olive Thomas: The Life and Death of a Silent Film Beauty* (Jefferson, NC: McFarland & Company, 2007).

Mary Pickford, *Sunshine and Shadow* (Garden City, NY: Doubleday, 1955), 197–99.

George Strum, Letter to the Editor, *New York Times*, June 1, 1997.

CHAPTER TWO: THE PALACE THEATRE

Anthony Slide, *The Encyclopedia of Vaudeville* (Jackson: University Press of Mississippi, 2012), 280.

Marian Spitzer, *The Palace: The Lively and Intimate Story of the Theater That Became a Legend* (New York: Atheneum, 1969).

"Acrobat Plunges to Palace Stage," *New York Times*, August 28, 1935.

"The Four Casting Pearls," *Santa Cruz Evening News*, August 28, 1935.

Jennifer Ashley Tepper, *The Untold Stories of Broadway: Volume 2* (Hood River, OR: Dress Circle Publishing, 2014).

"The Palace Theatre's Gang of Ghosts," *Ghosts and Murders Blog*, March 8, 2013.

Frank DiLella, "Touring Broadway's Haunted Past," *Spectrum News/NY1*, October 27, 2017.

CHAPTER THREE: THE BELASCO THEATRE

"David Belasco Dies; Dean of Theatre, 76, Had Long Been Ill," *New York Times*, May 15, 1931.

Isa Goldberg, "Broadway's Haunted Houses," *TheatreMania*, October 31, 2011.

Louis Botto, "Haunted Houses," *Playbill*, 1223, no. 2 (2007).

Robert Viagas, "The Real-Life Ghost Stories behind Broadway's 9 Haunted Theatres," *Playbill* (2013).

Barbara Hoffman, "Belasco's Spirit Is Making His Theatre a . . . Haunted House," *New York Post*, July 26, 2003.

Nick Paumgarten, "Relics: A Broadway Haunt," *The New Yorker*, July 3, 2006.

CHAPTER FOUR: THE AL HIRSCHFELD THEATRE AND THE ST. JAMES THEATRE

Arthur Frank Wertheim, *Vaudeville Wars: How the Keith-Albee and Orpheum Circuits Controlled the Big-Time and Its Performers* (New York: Palgrave Macmillan, 2006).

"Martin Beck Dies; Theatre Veteran; Manager, Producer and Actor, Builder of the Palace, Stricken Here at 71 Began Orpheum Circuit Headed Variety Group in West for 27 Years—Came to U.S. as Immigrant at 18," *New York Times*, November 17, 1940.

Philip Schoenberg, *Ghosts of Manhattan: Legendary Spirits and Notorious Haunts* (Charleston, SC: Haunted America, 2009).

CHAPTER FIVE: OTHER BROADWAY GHOSTS

Cindy Adams, "'The Visit' Crew Thinks Fosse's Ghost Lives in Broadway Theatre," *New York Post*, April 5, 2015.

Martha G., "Broadway Ghosts—The 5 Most Terrifyingly Haunted Theatres," *Experience First*, November 15, 2016.

Haunted Broadway, *Broadway Up Close: The Ghostlight Tour.*

"Scandals and Secrets of the Supernatural: The Stories behind Broadway's Haunted Theatres," *Playbill*, October 28, 2016, https://www.playbill.com/article/scandals-and-secrets-of-the

-supernatural-the-stories-behind-broadways-haunted-theatres
-com-368882.

Sarah Crocker, "The Creepiest Stories of Broadway Ghosts," Grunge
.com, February 2, 2021.

Robert Viagas, ed., *The Playbill Broadway Yearbook 2004–2005* (New
York: Playbill Books/Applause Books, 2005).

Robert Viagas, ed., *The Playbill Broadway Yearbook 2005–2006* (New
York: Playbill Books/Applause Books, 2006).

Robert Viagas, ed., *The Playbill Broadway Yearbook 2008–2009* (New
York: Playbill Books/Applause Books, 2009).

Robert Viagas, ed., *The Playbill Broadway Yearbook 2010–2011* (New
York: Playbill Books/Applause Books, 2011).

Robert Viagas, ed., *The Playbill Broadway Yearbook 2011–2012* (New
York: Playbill Books/Applause Books, 2012).

Robert Viagas, ed., *The Playbill Broadway Yearbook 2012–2013* (New
York: Playbill Books/Applause Books, 2013).

Robert Viagas, ed., *The Playbill Broadway Yearbook 2013–2014* (New
York: Playbill Books/Applause Books, 2014).

Robert Viagas, "The Real-Life Ghost Stories Behind Broadway's 9
Haunted Theatres," *Playbill*, 2013.

Louis Botto, "Haunted Houses," *Playbill* 1223, no. 2 (2007).

Becki Robins, "Why People See Ghosts, According to Science," *Grunge*,
April 21, 2020.

CHAPTER SIX: CELEBRITY GHOST STORIES

Louis Botto, "Haunted Houses," *Playbill* 1223, no. 2 (2007).

Michael Buckley, "Celeste Holm," *TheatreWeek*, May 6, 1991.

Lydia Price, "Celebs Who Have Had Actual Ghost Encounters," *People*, updated December 22, 2021.

Stephen Adams, "Patrick Stewart Saw Ghost Performing *Waiting for Godot*," *The Telegraph*, August 25, 2009.

Robert Viagas, ed., *The Playbill Broadway Yearbook 2005–2006* (New York: Playbill Books/Applause Books, 2006).

Louis Botto, *At This Theatre* (New York: Playbill Books/Applause Books, 2000).

CHAPTER SEVEN: OFF-BROADWAY GHOSTS

L'Aura Hladik, *Ghosthunting New York City* (Cincinnati, OH: Clerisy Press, 2010).

Philip Schoenberg, *Ghosts of Manhattan: Legendary Spirits and Notorious Haunts* (Charleston, SC: Haunted America, 2009).

Mervyn Rothstein, "A New Show in and about a Theatre with a Past," *New York Times*, February 16, 1990.

Rebecca Groves, "Sighting Ghosts: The Theatrical Spectrality of History, Identity and Politics in Mac Wellman's *Crowbar*," Academia.edu., 2002, https://www.academia.edu/4090372/Si_gh_ting_Ghost s_The_Theatrical_Spectrality_of_History_Identity_and_Politics _in_Mac_Wellmans_Crowbar_2002.

CHAPTER EIGHT: HAUNTED U.S. THEATRES OF THE EAST

Marshall Everett, *Chicago's Awful Theater Horror* (Staten Island, NY: Memorial Publishing Company, 1904).

Jason Zasky, "Burning Down the House: The 1903 Iroquois Theater Fire," *Failure Magazine*, October 1, 2009.

Francine Uenuma, "The Iroquois Theater Disaster Killed Hundreds and Changed Fire Safety Forever," *Smithsonian Magazine*, June 12, 2018.

[Story on the Iroquois Theatre fire], *New York Times*, January 5, 1904.

Nat Brandt, *Chicago Death Trap: The Iroquois Theatre Fire of 1903* (Carbonsdale: Southern Illinois University Press, 2003).

Anthony P. Hatch, *Tinder Box: The Iroquois Theatre Disaster* (Chicago: Academy Chicago Publishers,1903).

Pamela Whitehead, "Who's That Pale Guy in the Crowd Scene?" *Washington Post*, October 27, 1978.

Marjoria B. Garber, *Profiling Shakespeare* (New York: Routledge, 2008).

Michael Norman and Beth Scott, "Ford's Theatre," Haunted America, April 3, 2013.

Virginia Lamkin, "Haunted Ford's Theatre," *Seeks Ghosts* (blog), April 3, 2013.

Thomas A. Bogar, *American Presidents Attend the Theatre* (Jefferson, NC: McFarland & Company, 2006).

Thomas A. Bogar, *Backstage at the Lincoln Assassination: The Untold Story of the Actors and Stagehands at Ford's Theatre.* (Washington, DC: Regenery History, 2013).

Adam Selzer, *Ghosts of Lincoln: Discovering His Paranormal Legacy* (Woodbury, MN: Llewellyn Publications, 2015).

Sam Baltrusis, *Ghosts of Boston: Haunts of the Hub* (Charleston SC: Haunted America/The History Press, 2012).

Holly Mascott Nadler, *Ghosts of Boston Town: Three Centuries of True Hauntings* (Camden, ME: Down East Books, 2002).

Chris Woodyard, *Ghostly Tales from the Buckeye State*. (Dayton, OH: Kestrel Publications, 1991).

Lisa Powell and Vivienne Machi, "Ghostly Faces and Strange Noises Are among the Hauntings at Dayton's Historic Theater," *Dayton Daily News*, October 26, 2020.

Tom Szaroleta, "Florida Theatre's 'Ghost' Seats Will Be Preserved," *Florida Times-Union*, August 10, 2020.

Troy Taylor, *Haunted Decatur: 25th Anniversary Edition: Two Centuries of Decatur's Spirits, Scandals, and Sins* (Independently published, 2020).

Andrew DaRosa, "Haunted Connecticut: A Guide to the Spookiest, Most Haunted Places in the State," *Connecticut Post*, September 25, 2020.

Barbara Smith, *Haunted Theatres* (Edmonton, AB: Ghost House Books, 2003).

William Dennis Hauck, *The Haunted Directory* (New York: Puffin, 2002).

Vincent Astor, "Orpheum Ghost Stories," YouTube, October 29, 2012, https://www.youtube.com/watch?v=EWrFq0XLcNg.

Matthew Zeak, "Haunted Mishler Theatre: 12 Year Old Tells Her Ghostly Tale," Pennsylvania Mountains of Attractions, 2010, http://www.pennsylvania-mountains-of-attractions.com/ghostly.html.

Valerie Fraser Luesse, "The Orpheum Theatre in Memphis Has a Resident Ghost," *Southern Living Magazine*, https://sports.yahoo.com/orpheum-theatre-memphis-resident-ghost-173540659.html.

Alan Brown, *Haunted Places in the American South* (Jackson: University Press of Mississippi, 2002).

Kym Clark, "Orpheum Ghost Stories with Vincent Astor," Action News 5, August 18, 2021.

Kym Clark, "5 Star Stories: Spirits Sharing the Show at the Orpheum Theatre," Action News 5, 2021.

Beppie Noyes, *Mosby, the Kennedy Center Cat: A True Story Made Legend* (Norwell, MA: VP Books, 1978).

Sarah Booth Conroy, "Tailing the Famous Kennedy Center Cat," *Washington Post*, November 3, 1998.

Michael S. Rosenwald "The 'Feline Spook of the Capitol': How a Demon Cat Became Washington's Best Ghost Story," *Washington Post*, October 31, 2018.

CHAPTER NINE: HAUNTED U.S. THEATRES OF THE WEST

"Ghosts of the Pantages Theatre," Totally L.A., March 11, 2018, https://totally-la.com/ghosts-pantages-theatre/#.

Micaela Cummings, "The Eternal House Staff," Broadway in Hollywood, October 31, 2017.

Mark Moran and Mark Sceurman, *Weird U.S.: Your Travel Guide to America's Local Legends and Best Kept Secrets* by (New York: Sterling Books, 2005).

"The Palace Theatre History," Los Angeles Theatre.

Bob Thomas, *Clown Prince of Hollywood: The Antic Life and Times of Jack L. Warner* (New York: McGraw-Hill, 1990), 11.

Marianne McClary, "Haunted Sacramento: Where Do the Ghosts Roam in California's Capital?," CBS Sacramento. October 29, 2018.

Bill Underwood, "The Old Lady Lives On: Brady Theater Continues to Bring Big Acts after More Than 82 Years," *Tulsa World*, March 6,

1996, https://tulsaworld.com/archive/the-old-lady-lives-on
-brady-theater-continues-to-bring-big-acts-after-more-than/
article_b16c33df-5c4b-5487-90f4-a1f0dffd5ae8.html, updated
February 27, 2019.

Kathy Weiser, *Legends of America* (Legends of America Books, May
2017).

Cindy Sutter, "'Colorado X: Case Files of the Paranormal'
Investigates Macky 'Ghost,'" *Colorado Daily Sentinel*, July
12, 1966, https://www.coloradodaily.com/2009/08/16/
colorado-x-case-files-of-the-paranormal-investigates-macky-ghost/.

"Signature Theatres Dole Cannery 18," PANICd, https://www.panicd
.com/signature-theatres-dole-cannery-18.html.

"Roseland Theatre," US Ghost Adventures, January 30, 2022, https://
usghostadventures.com/.

Lacey Womack, "Phantom of the Opera: 10 Haunted Theaters
throughout the World," The Travel, November 5, 2019, https://
www.thetravel.com/haunted-theaters-throughout-world/.

CHAPTER TEN: THE GHOSTS OF LONDON'S THEATRES

Andrew Dickinson, "Inside the World's Most Haunted Theatre," *The
Guardian*, October 29, 2015.

"Grimaldi's Ghost" The International Society for the Study of Ghosts
and Apparitions. New York.

Thomas Scott, *The Bric a Brac Shop* podcast, YouTube, https://www
.youtube.com/c/TheBricaBracShop.

Michael Coveney and Peter Dazely, *London Theatres* (London: Francie
& Finch, 2020).

"The Terriss Tragedy, *New York Dramatic Mirror*, December 21, 1897.

Jim De Young and John Miller, *London Theatre Walks: Thirteen Dramatic Tours through Four Centuries of History and Legend* (New York: Applause Books, 2003).

"Halloween Stories," Oldvictheatre.com, October 31, 2018, https://www.oldvictheatre.com/news/2018/10/halloween-stories. Link no longer available.

Zoe Paskett, "The Most Haunted Theatres in London's West End" *Evening Standard*, October 25, 2018.

"Spooky CCTV Footage Captures Ghost at Theatre," *Metro*, July 29, 2014.

CHAPTER ELEVEN: OTHER INTERNATIONAL GHOSTS

Alexander Laing, ed., *Great Ghost Stories of the World, The Haunted Omnibus* (Garden City, NY: Garden City Publishing Company, 1939), 278–79.

"A Ghost at the Garnier Opera House of Paris?," Prometour, October 10, 2018, https://prometour.com/a-ghost-at-the-garnier-opera-house-of-paris/.

Liam Rudden, "Chilling Encounters with Albert, the Ghost of the Edinburgh Playhouse," *Edinburgh News*, July 4, 2020.

Alison Campsie, "Terrifying Tales from Scotland's Most Haunted Theatres," *The Scotsman*, October 30, 2019.

"The Dark Side of Milan: Ghosts, Legends and All the Spookiest Places in the City," Milanairports.com, October 31, 2018, https://www.milanairports.com/en/around-milan/dark-side-of-milan.

Todd Huizenga, "Raising the Dead: And a Few Questions—with Maria Callas' Hologram," NPR, November 6, 2018, https://www.npr.org/sections/deceptivecadence/2018/11/06/664653353/raising-the-dead-and-a-few-questions-with-maria-callas-hologram.

"Haunted Alberta: Ghost Stories from All around the Province," *The Huffington Post Alberta*, May 12, 2013, updated October 30, 2015, https://www.huffpost.com/archive/ca/entry/haunted-alberta-ghost-stories_n_3262819.

Michelle Butterfield, "Haunted Edmonton: 9 Spooky Places That Will Scare Your Socks Off," *The Huffington Post*, October 21, 2016, https://www.huffpost.com/archive/ca/entry/haunted-places-edmonton_n_12591078.

"Ghost Stories from Melbourne's Princess Theatre," *What's On Melbourne*, April 15, 2016, https://whatsonblog.melbourne.vic.gov.au/ghost-stories-from-melbournes-princess-theatre/.

"Shocking Occurrence at the Princess's Theatre: Tragic Death of Mr. Federici," *The Argus* (Melbourne), March 5, 1888, 8.

"Production of *Faust* in Melbourne," *The Press* 45, no. 7025 (March 29, 1888), 3.

Graeme Blundell, "Marvellous Melbourne," *The Age*, August 27–28, 2005.

Howie Severino, "The Manila Film Center Mystery: A Ghostly Place or an Urban Legend?," November 1, 2005.

Nicai De Guzman, "The Mysterious Curse of the Manila Film Center," *Esquire Philippines*, November 7, 2019.

Lisa Waller Rogers, "Lisa's History Room: Imelda Marcos: The 'Mine' Girl," Lisawallerrogers.com, March 31, 2010, https://lisawallerrogers.com/2010/03/31/imelda-marcos-the-mine-girl/.

Davie McGill, *Full Circle: The History of the St. James Theatre* (Wellington, NZ: Phantom House Books, 1997).

"Peter Jackson's Ghostly Encounter," *New Zealand Stuff*, November 26, 2009.

CHAPTER TWELVE: GHOSTS OF THE PAST

Barbara Smith, *Haunted Theaters* (Edmonton, AB: Ghost House Books, 2002).

"Broadway Up Close: The Ghostlight Tour," Haunted Broadway, https://www.broadwayupclose.com/ghostlighttour.

Brooks Atkinson, *Broadway* (New York: Atheneum, 1970).

ChillyStories.com.

"The Ghost Haunt Goes When Wallacks' Goes," *New York Times*, April 25, 1915.

"Dear Showbill," *Playbill*, September 1983.

Theodore Barber, *Phantasmagorical Wonders: The Magic Lantern Ghost Show in Nineteenth-Century America* (Bloomington: Indiana University Press, 1989), 73–75.

CHAPTER THIRTEEN: LITERARY GHOST STORIES

Robert Douglas-Fairhurst, ed., *A Christmas Carol and Other Christmas Books* (Oxford: Oxford University Press, 2006).

Bibliography

Adams, Charles J. III. *Philadelphia Ghost Stories.* Reading, PA: Exeter House Books, 2012.

Anger, Kenneth. *Hollywood Babylon.* New York: Straight Arrow Press/Simon & Schuster, 1975.

Atkinson, Brooks. *Broadway.* New York: Atheneum, 1970.

Baltrusis, Sam. *Ghosts of Boston: Haunts of the Hub.* Charleston SC: Haunted America/The History Press, 2012.

Barber, Theodore. *Phantasmagorical Wonders: The Magic Lantern Ghost Show in Nineteenth-Century America.* Bloomington: Indiana University Press, 1989.

Blum, Deborah. *Ghost Hunters: William James and the Search for Scientific Proof of Life after Death.* New York: Penguin, 2006.

Bogar, Thomas A. *American Presidents Attend the Theatre.* Jefferson, NC: McFarland & Company, 2006.

———. *Backstage at the Lincoln Assassination: The Untold Story of the Actors and Stagehands at Ford's Theatre.* Washington, DC: Regenery History, 2013.

Brandt, Nat. *Chicago Death Trap: The Iroquois Theatre Fire of 1903.* Carbonsdale: Southern Illinois University Press, 2003.

Bromley, Nick. *Stage Ghosts and Haunted Theatres.* London: LNP Books, 2021.

Brown, Alan. *Haunted Places in the American South.* Jackson: University Press of Mississippi, 2002.

Carlson, Marvin. *The Haunted Stage: The Theatre as Memory Machine.* Ann Arbor: University of Michigan Press, 2003.

De Young, Jim, and John Miller. *London Theatre Walks: Thirteen Dramatic Tours through Four Centuries of History and Legend.* New York: Applause Books, 2003.

Dwyer, Jeff. *Ghost Hunter's Guide to Los Angeles.* Gretna, LA: Pelican Publishing Company, , 2007.

Enders, Jody. *Death by Drama and Other Medieval Urban Legends.* Chicago: University of Chicago Press, 2002.

Everett, Marshall. *Chicago's Awful Theater Horror.* Staten Island, NY: Memorial Publishing Company, 1904.

Frethem, Deborah. *Ghost Stories of St. Petersburg, Clearwater and Pinellas County.* Charleston, SC: Haunted America, 2007.

Haining, Peter, ed. *Greasepaint and Ghosts.* London: William Kimber, 1981.

Hatch, Anthony P. *Tinder Box: The Iroquois Theatre Disaster.* Chicago: Academy Chicago Publishers,1903.

Hauck, Dennis William. *Haunted Places: The National Directory.* New York: Penguin, 2002.

———. *The Haunted Directory.* New York: Puffin, 2002.

Henderson, Mary C. *The New Amsterdam: The Biography of a Broadway Theatre.* Disney Enterprises Inc., 1997.

Hladik, L'Aura. *Ghosthunting in New York City.* Cincinnati, OH: Clerisy Press, 2010.

Jacobson, Laurie, and Marc Wanamaker. *Hollywood Haunted: A Ghostly Tour of Filmland.* Santa Monica, CA: Angel City Press, 1994.

King, Stephen. *Stephen King's Danse Macabre.* New York: Berkley Books, 1981.

Laing, Alexander, ed. *Great Ghost Stories of the World, The Haunted Omnibus.* Garden City, NY: Garden City Publishing Company,1939.

Leslie, F. Andrew *The Haunting of Hill House.* New York: Dramatists Play Service, 1992.

Marsolais, Ken, Roger McFarlane, and Tom Viola. *Broadway Day and Night: Backstage and Behind the Scenes.* New York: Pocket Books, 1992.

McGill, Davie. *Full Circle: The History of the St. James Theatre.* Wellington, NZ: Phantom House Books, 1997.

Michael Coveney and Peter Dazely. *London Theatres* (New Edition). London, U.K.: Francie & Finch, October 6, 2020.

Moran, Mark, and Mark Sceurman. *Weird U.S.: Your Travel Guide to America's Local Legends and Best Kept Secrets.* New York: Sterling Books, 2005.

Nadler, Holly Mascott. *Ghosts of Boston Town: Three Centuries of True Hauntings.* Camden, ME: Down East Books, 2002.

Noyes, Beppie. *Mosby, the Kennedy Center Cat.* Norwell MA: VSP Books, 1978.

Ogden, Tom. *Haunted Theatres: Playhouse Phantoms, Opera House Horrors, and Backstage Banshees.* Gob Pile Press, 2009.

Pickford, Mary. *Sunshine and Shadow.* Garden City, NY: Doubleday, 1955.

Rich, Frank. *Ghost Light: A Memoir.* New York: Random House, 2000.

Schoenberg, Philip. *Ghosts of Manhattan: Legendary Spirits and Notorious Haunts.* Charleston, SC: Haunted America, 2009.

Selzer, Adam. *Ghosts of Lincoln: Discovering His Paranormal Legacy.* Woodbury MN: Llewellyn Publications, 2015.

Slide, Anthony. *The Encyclopedia of Vaudeville* by Jackson: University Press of Mississippi, 2012.

Smith, Barbara. *Haunted Theatres.* Edmonton, AB: Ghost House Books, 2003.

Sondheim, Stephen (lyrics), and Laurents, Arthur (libretto). *Romeo and Juliet and West Side Story.* New York: Laurel Leaf/Random House, 1965.

Spitzer, Marian. *The Palace: The Lively and Intimate Story of the Theater That Became a Legend.* New York: Atheneum, 1969.

Sutton Vane. *Outward Bound.* London: Samuel French, 1924.

Taylor, Troy. *Flickering Images: The History and Hauntings of the Avon Theatre.* Alton, IL: Whitchapel Productions Press, 2001.

———. *Haunted Decatur: 25th Anniversary Edition: Two Centuries of Decatur's Spirits, Scandals, and Sins.* Independently published, 2020.

———. *Hell Hath No Fury: 13 Spirits of the Wicked and the Wronged.* Jacksonville, IL: American Hauntings Ink, 2021.

Tepper, Jennifer Ashley. *The Untold Stories of Broadway: Volume 2.* Hood River, OR: Dress Circle Publishing, 2014.

Thomas, Bob. *Clown Prince of Hollywood: The Antic Life and Times of Jack L. Warner.* New York: McGraw-Hill, 1990.

Viagas, Robert, ed. *The Playbill Broadway Yearbook.* New York: Playbill Books/Applause Books, 2005–2015.

Viagas, Robert, and Louis Botto. *At This Theatre: 110 Years of Broadway Shows, Stories and Stars.* New York: Applause Books, 2010.

Viertel, Jack. *The Secret Life of the American Musical: How Broadway Shows Are Built.* New York: Farrar, Straus & Giroux, 2016.

Vogel, Michelle. *Olive Thomas: The Life and Death of a Silent Film Beauty.* Jefferson, NC: McFarland & Company, 2007.

Wertheim, Arthur Frank. *Vaudeville Wars: How the Keith-Albee and Orpheum Circuits Controlled the Big-Time and Its Performers.* New York: Palgrave Macmillan, 2006.

Wilder, Thornton. *Our Town: A Play in Three Acts.* New York: Harper Perennial Modern Classics: A Reissue Edition, 2020.

Woodyard, Chris. *Ghostly Tales from the Buckeye State.* Dayton: Haunted Ohio, 1991.

Young, June Hurley. *The Don Ce-Sar Story.* St. Petersburgh, FL: Partnership Press, 2007.

Index

Page references for photos are italicized.